LEAD
SUCCESS

LEARN THE ESSENTIALS OF
TRUE LEADERSHIP

LEAD 4 SUCCESS

LEARN THE ESSENTIALS OF
TRUE LEADERSHIP

George Hallenbeck
With CCL Associates

Center for
Creative
Leadership

LEAD CONTRIBUTOR
George Hallenbeck

DIRECTOR OF ASSESSMENTS, TOOLS, AND PUBLICATIONS
Sylvester Taylor

MANAGER, PUBLICATION DEVELOPMENT
Peter Scisco

EDITOR
Stephen Rush

ASSOCIATE EDITOR
Shaun Martin

DESIGN, LAYOUT, AND COVER DESIGN
Ed Morgan, navybluedesign.com

RIGHTS AND PERMISSIONS
Kelly Lombardino

EDITORIAL BOARD
David Altman, Elaine Biech, Regina Eckert, Joan Gurvis, Jennifer Habig, Kevin Liu, Neal Maillet, Jennifer Martineau, Portia Mount, Laura Santana

CCL No. 001005 – Print
CCL No. 001005e – Ebook

978-1-60491-644-7 – Print
978-1-60491-645-4 – Ebook

Center for Creative Leadership
www.ccl.org

Acknowledgements: Special thanks and acknowledgement go to two individuals. To Jeff Howard, for his vision and support for this book project and the larger Lead 4 Success initiative of which it is a part. To Peter Scisco, for his editorial acumen and willingness to be agile in the face of the many moving parts, sudden shifts, and CCL "firsts" that characterized this project, including its breakneck pace.
Thanks also to the many people who put their time, skill, and effort toward this publication, including: Lorraine Ahearn, Ed Morgan, Martin Wilcox, Jamie Velez, Stephen Martin, Jeff Anderson, Portia Mount, Davida Sharpe, Amanda Fonorow, Felecia Corbett, Dave Skinner, Kris Downing, and Kelly Lombardino. And last but not least, gratitude to the many CCL faulty whose works informed much of this book's content.

Finally, I am grateful for the love, support, and understanding of my family, especially my wife Kate, who over ten years and seven titles has dealt with late nights and weekends of writing, "book brain," and other highs and lows of the book writing process.

CONTENTS

FOREWORD

Well into my career in the U.S. Navy, I found myself on an unexpected trans-Atlantic flight that cut into already scarce time with my family. Worn out, I'd just settled into my seat when a flight attendant approached and asked me to swap seats with another passenger who was uncomfortable in hers. Grudgingly, I agreed.

Moving toward the front, I saw a woman, pale as a ghost, rush past and take my old seat. A few steps later, the source of her distress became clear.

In the seat next to the one she had just abandoned sat a young woman with no arms or legs, who was obviously shaken by how her appearance had rattled her previous seat mate. "Hello," I said. "Hopefully, you won't mind sitting next to an old Navy guy for this whole flight."

The conversation we had as our plane crossed the ocean was unforgettable. This extraordinary young woman explained how she had been given up for adoption at birth and taken in by another family that lovingly treated her as if she had no disabilities at all. Her parents expected her to do the same thing her able-bodied siblings did—use her gifts, confront and overcome challenges, learn from mistakes, get an education, and be a leader. At this moment, she was an engineer on the way to her first international conference.

Her inspiring story has much to teach us all—and it underscores the theme of this book: our experiences offer us immense opportunities to grow as individuals and leaders, but only if we fully embrace the good and bad in them and diligently apply the lessons learned. Like my young friend, if we possess the necessary skills to learn from and act on what happens to us every day, we have a much greater chance of making a positive impact on everyone around us.

Center for Creative Leadership (CCL) believes we need four essential skills in order to learn from experience and lead successfully—self-awareness, learning agility, communication, and influence. At CCL, we believe that everyone has the potential to be a leader. This practical and engaging book is your guide for getting there and for staying committed to getting better every day.

John Ryan
President & CEO at Center for Creative Leadership

. . . .

THE JOURNEY AWAITS:

THE OPPORTUNITY OF EXPERIENCE

In the summer of 2016 a funny thing happened on the way to the vending machine. Bottled water bypassed carbonated soft drinks as the top-selling beverage for the first time since . . . well, carbonated soft drinks. For a multinational company like PepsiCo, whose flagship cola brand is second only to the iconic Coke, this surely spelled disaster.

Didn't it?

On the plus side, PepsiCo owned about two dozen billion-dollar brands, from Diet Mountain Dew to Doritos. On the minus side— and a big minus it was—soda sales had dipped lower every year for a decade and showed no sign of turning around. How was it then that, in 2016, PepsiCo remained the largest food company in North America and one of the most admired and profitable brands in the world?

The answer, in large part, was leadership and vision from the top that was driven by an ability to learn from experience, apply those lessons, and clearly communicate them to influence others. PepsiCo CEO Indra Nooyi charted a long-term course for the company to navigate a change even greater than the impacts of globalization or economic downturns. That change was consumer trends, driven by a kaleidoscope of conflicting desires.

The picture was endlessly complicated. Drinks and snacks needed to taste good but without the calories. Then again, consumers distrusted diet substitutes. They wanted treats that were appealing and convenient but also nutritious. Variety and novelty had instant allure. But there was a contradictory pull toward the nostalgic, classic, and handmade, hearkening back to the first batch of Pepsi produced in the late 1800s behind the soda fountain counter in a small-town American drugstore. In other words, consumers wanted it all.

As if that weren't a sufficiently tall order, the modern-day PepsiCo sought to present itself as ethical, environmentally responsible, culturally diverse, and health-conscious. This was more than public relations or brand marketing. It was survival. What was good for the customers, as Nooyi saw it, was good for the business. If consumer tastes went through such dramatic change every two to three years, PepsiCo needed the ability to change with them.

Thus, a company that had been as conventionally American as hot dogs—and offered comparable nutritional benefits—had now expanded its menu to include packaged kale smoothies, whole-grain pita crisps, purified water, and individual servings of garlic hummus. Nooyi, a business strategist who joined PepsiCo in 1994 and was named CEO 12 years later, meanwhile articulated a set of goals she termed

"PERFORMANCE WITH PURPOSE,"

promoting a progressive corporate agenda on everything from sustainable water use to professional development.

PEPSICO

How Nooyi gained the social capital to help PepsiCo reinvent itself is a textbook case of experience-driven leadership. The move to diversify PepsiCo beyond its traditional products that were "fun for you," as Nooyi termed them, to foods that were "good for you" was the most ambitious transformation she had been part of, but it was not the first. That fact underlines an important premise of the Center for Creative Leadership's approach:

LEADERS ARE NOT BORN, BUT MADE.

At such a critical juncture, changemakers like Nooyi need to harness the mindset, behaviors, and tools that successful leaders draw upon every day, capabilities that subsequent chapters of this book will explore in depth. Four fundamental skills drive the thoughts and actions of the most effective leaders:

SELF-AWARENESS—an understanding of their identity and what they have to offer

LEARNING AGILITY—the capacity to absorb new information, process it, and use it to meet new challenges quickly and decisively

COMMUNICATION—the ability to establish shared understanding with others and convey a vision for addressing challenges

INFLUENCE—the power to persuade others to act on that vision

But let's step back a moment to consider a fundamental question:

WHERE AND HOW DO LEADERS OBTAIN THESE EXTRAORDINARY SKILLS?

The answer, as we'll learn, is that experience-driven leaders like Nooyi have often been fashioning them all along.

THE ITINERARY of
EXPERIENCE

Leadership-building experiences didn't happen to Nooyi by accident. She sought them out. Born in India and educated in Calcutta, she worked for multinational companies in her native country and then applied to management school at Yale as one of its first MBAs. Her motivation was to encounter a new world, and she brought a mentality of open-mindedness, curiosity, continual learning, and on-the-ground street smarts.

This meant doing more than studying in the United States; she immersed herself in its culture. For example, Nooyi, who loved the game of cricket, turned her attention to baseball. She immersed herself in the New York Yankees and their team statistics. If a person wanted to communicate, she told her biographer years later, this required learning both the language and what people talked about. At the same time, Nooyi learned not to hide her identity and what made her.

After an awkward and self-conscious first job interview, to which she wore an ill-fitting western suit, she went to her second interview wearing a sari, and landed a job as a strategy consultant. Aware that she was an outsider in a predominantly white, male, Anglo-Saxon, American-born corporate setting, Nooyi set out to leverage what she brought to the table as an Indian-born Hindu woman with a global perspective.

The 1980s in some ways foreshadowed today's tumultuous business climate. Companies that had been successful for years doing things the way they had always done them could no longer operate that way. This was true for Motorola, where Nooyi worked next, at a time when the venerable TV and radio manufacturer found itself on the cusp of a communications revolution.

Motorola introduced to the public what now seems an antiquated device:

THE PAGER.

Popular with emergency-room physicians and others whose jobs kept them mobile, the small devices presaged the cellular technology boom and the sweeping changes to come with mobile technology. By definition, successful innovation was fleeting. To remain on top in the volatile telecommunications industry, Motorola had to keep moving. A case in point:

WHEN WAS THE LAST TIME YOU SAW A PAGER?

By the time Nooyi had worked her way up to CEO at PepsiCo in 2006, standing still was even less an option. Sales at the soda and snack colossus were falling in key markets—in some areas, drastically. Adding to the uncertainty were new regulations on snacks and drinks. The company had a choice: The first, what Nooyi called the "pedal to the metal" option, was to slash costs and opt for short-term profits. The wiser choice, she convinced PepsiCo's board, was to pursue a long-term strategy by broadening the company portfolio and developing new capabilities.

For a business essentially built on instant gratification, this was a radical switch. It required awareness and understanding of the past, and the continued appeal of core products, while maintaining a constant eye to the future and how that core was evolving.

In a sense, Nooyi was drawing on earlier experience in introducing sweeping change to PepsiCo. As CFO, she had helped persuade the company to spin off subsidiaries Taco Bell, KFC, and Pizza Hut—restaurant brands that were struggling and did not mesh with PepsiCo's packaged food identity—and then had helped PepsiCo begin to rebuild the company's net worth by acquiring Tropicana. Rather than see the restaurants as a loss, Nooyi helped the company to see them as an opportunity to regroup in a new direction.

SECRETS of the
EARLY RISER

For a woman who had grown up in Madras, India, and risen each day with the rest of her family at 4:00 a.m., both the taco, fried chicken, and pizza division and the snack and drink division at PepsiCo held an obvious gap: breakfast. None of the products was relevant until late morning, and Nooyi understood that the company's sales were dormant for too many hours out of the day, missing an opportunity.

In arguing for the restaurant spinoff, Nooyi and then-CEO Roger Enrico laid out facts so compelling that board members felt they had arrived at the decision on their own. How Nooyi approached that change later informed the arduous task of taking PepsiCo in a future direction. With employees, she held a series of open-forum meetings to communicate the strategy and hear feedback. With managers, she made the urgency and the high stakes clear. They would have two to three years to make the change, but they had to change in order for the company to survive. Otherwise, she noted wryly, they would all be having retirement parties.

No change so sweeping happens in a straight line or without setbacks and frustrations, and Nooyi's approach took that into account. The company mantra was to learn to tolerate failure as a way to unleash innovation, just as the struggle with the restaurants had opened up the expansion with Tropicana. In some ways, this new journey meant that the huge multinational had to act like a small startup, discovering ways to launch experimental products in test markets such as China and Japan (think cucumber-flavored Pepsi) and give them three months to succeed or to pull the plug and move on to the next idea.

In an atmosphere of innovation, Nooyi gave employees the tools to think in new ways, for example starting a design department that looked well beyond logos and packaging to how consumers reacted to products and interacted with them.

Even if customers pined for the "real sugar" in throwback Pepsi bottles such as the nostalgic 1893, the truth was that the traditional soda dispenser at fast-food restaurants had to appeal to an iPhone generation. The company developed a new dispenser that resembles an oversized iPad that talks to consumers, displays pictures of the drinks as they are being mixed, and saves favorites to a swipe card. The mammoth company learned to sweat the small stuff. Was an individual Sunchip small enough to pop in your mouth? Was a 24-pack of Aquafina light enough for the average shopper to heft into a grocery cart?

It was a mindset that constantly processed and applied experience. "Every morning," Nooyi told the *Harvard Business Review* in 2015, "you've got to wake up with a healthy fear that the world is changing, and a conviction that, to win, you have to change faster and be more agile than anyone else."

THE RICH RELEVANCE of
EXPERIENCE

What we can learn from leaders like Nooyi and other leaders featured in this book is how to look at challenges in a different way, how to see them as opportunities and as points where we can apply the lessons from our unique set of past experiences in novel, innovative ways.

The goal of the following pages is to assist you in thinking about your own story and the leadership lessons it holds and in understanding experience as a source of great opportunity for becoming a more effective leader. You will explore:

A MINDSET THAT HELPS YOU ANTICIPATE AND SEEK OUT LEARNING OPPORTUNITIES

. . . .

A SKILLSET THAT HELPS YOU TO ASK QUESTIONS AND LOOK AT PROBLEMS IN NEW WAYS

. . . .

A TOOLSET FOR GAINING WISDOM FROM PAST EXPERIENCES AND APPLYING IT TO NEW CHALLENGES

We have a rich itinerary and a rewarding destination ahead.

LET'S GET STARTED.

THE FUNDAMENTALS of
EXPERIENCE-DRIVEN LEADERSHIP

The question you might have right now is, "Where do I begin?"

Consider this section your pre-journey orientation, where we'll lay a foundation of understanding that will help you develop into an experience-driven leader.

. . . .

CHAPTER 1 introduces you to three fundamental truths we've learned from over 40 years of research into the role of experience in leadership development.

CHAPTER 2 highlights the Fundamental Four leadership skills essential to making the most of your experiences.

CHAPTER 3 merges all of this together into an integrated model of leadership that positions you to rediscover your past, seize your present, and shape your future.

. . . .

Your insights from these chapters will provide you with the understanding and context you'll need to make the most of the content in Sections II through IV. We encourage you to take the time to familiarize yourself with these fundamentals and refer back to them as necessary to guide your development.

CHAPTER ONE

THE THREE FUNDAMENTAL TRUTHS OF EXPERIENCE-DRIVEN LEADERSHIP

Experience is a vast territory. Fortunately, it is well-charted terrain. Since its inception in 1970 the Center for Creative Leadership (CCL) has researched the role of experience in leadership development. Along the way, CCL has identified some key principles that focus you on what matters most in becoming an experience-driven leader. We've also uncovered some common misunderstandings that might lead you down the wrong path.

Three fundamental truths form the basis for understanding and practicing experience-driven leadership:

- EXPERIENCE MATTERS—LEADERS ARE MADE, NOT BORN
- EXPERIENCE IS VARIABLE—NOT ALL EXPERIENCES ARE EQUAL
- EXPERIENCE IS THE PAST, PRESENT, AND FUTURE AT ONCE

These overarching principles reinforce the mindset and practices essential to becoming an experience-driven leader. As you set goals and create a plan for development, we invite you to revisit these truths to inform and support your journey.

TRUTH #1 EXPERIENCE MATTERS— LEADERS ARE MADE, NOT BORN

Not so long ago, little was known about the origins of successful leadership. A variety of innate abilities and underlying traits were examined, but no single one stood out as a definitive answer to explain what led to greatness in some and unrealized potential in others. Gradually, the focus shifted away from the notion that some leaders are "born with it" and we only needed to identify those with "the right stuff."

But if great leadership is not the product of some natural-born talent, then what is its source?

A breakthrough in our understanding came when CCL researchers posed a straightforward question to a large group of successful executives. They asked them to recall specific events in their careers that had an important effect on how they currently led and to identify what they learned from these events.

The insights that emerged from this landmark research, called the "Lessons of Experience" study, have left a lasting imprint on the study and practice of leadership development. The practical knowledge gained from the Lessons of Experience and the many related studies that continue to this day form the basis for much of what we'll share with you in this book.

Here are four key points that reinforce that, when it comes to developing as a leader, it's our experiences—and what we make of them—that matter most.

EXPERIENCE IS
THE BEST TEACHER

Score one for conventional wisdom. CCL research definitively shows that we learn more about becoming an effective leader from our experiences on the job than any other source of development. More than we get from specific guidance from bosses, colleagues, coaches, and others. More than what we receive from formal development opportunities such as corporate training and academic courses.

Experiences that stretch us and get us out of our comfort zones yield the greatest benefits for learning, development, and growth. That's what sticks with us and makes a difference when we're faced with altogether new challenges. If you're really looking to learn, the prescription is clear:

MAKE THESE CHALLENGING
LEARNING EXPERIENCES
A PART OF YOUR
EVERYDAY LIFE

THE VALUE OF
EXPERIENCE IS UNIVERSAL

The conclusions from the initial Lessons of Experience research were based on studying a rather specific population, almost entirely white male executives from North America. So naturally, the question that comes to mind is, "If that doesn't describe me, are the results still relevant?"

The answer is, yes. Several years of studies around the globe, with individuals of varying age, gender, and organizational role, confirm that the results of the original study apply to everyone. The power of learning from experience transcends any given demographic or line on the map. It's just a fundamental quality of how we learn. Learning from experience is for anybody and everybody.

YOUR EXPERIENCE IS UNIQUELY YOURS

Whether you're conscious of it or not, you are acquiring potentially valuable learning experiences throughout your career (more on the "potential" aspect in a moment). Some of those experiences, particularly those that take place in a team setting, such as a new product launch or an organizational task force, are shared by others. But some, such as coaching a struggling employee or restoring confidence in a disappointed client, are likely to be yours and yours alone.

As you progress in your career, you'll acquire your own unique portfolio of experiences. It may bear similarities to others', but it can't be duplicated. Think of it like your own experience DNA or fingerprint. That's very powerful because you can mine and apply your experience in a way that no one else can. And if you've acquired truly valuable learning experiences *and* you've made the most of them, you also have unique advantages in leveraging that accumulated experience.

SOME PEOPLE LEARN MORE
FROM EXPERIENCE THAN OTHERS

Just because you've had exposure to an experience that is rich in opportunities for learning doesn't necessarily guarantee that you're going to learn from it. Failing to fully appreciate the potential learning opportunity in an experience happens more often than you might realize: going through the motions, phoning it in, checking the boxes, playing it safe. Experience is only what you make of it.

Rather than all or nothing, most of us fall somewhere in the middle in terms of how we avail ourselves of experience. In most learning situations, we pick up some fundamental principles or rules of thumb, and we can say that we've grown a bit, but then we're on to the next experience. An unfortunate few people—and one or two examples likely come to mind pretty quickly for you—go through just about everything more or less unchanged.

BUT THEN THERE'S ALSO THE RELATIVE FEW WHO TAKE FULL ADVANTAGE OF THEIR LEARNING OPPORTUNITIES AND OFTEN COME AWAY SIGNIFICANTLY CHANGED.

Many factors contribute to the ability to learn from experience. Much of the rest of this book will introduce you to some of the essential skills that will help you become more savvy at learning from experience and then applying those lessons to help you take on new challenges.

"LIFE IS A LEARNING EXPERIENCE, ONLY IF YOU LEARN."
– YOGI BERRA

EXPERIENCE IS VARIABLE— NOT ALL EXPERIENCES ARE EQUAL

As just pointed out, people differ in their ability to learn from experience. And their experiences differ, too. If you become adept at sizing up which situations provide the greatest opportunity for learning and also teach you specific things you need to develop, then you will better position yourself to seize and make the most of those experiences.

Oftentimes it's the experience that at first glance seems unappealing, even downright scary, that actually has the most to offer. Mary Barra, the CEO of General Motors Company, shared this advice with up-and-coming leaders in her LinkedIn blog:

> "IN MY CASE, SOME OF MY MOST IMPORTANT CAREER LEARNING OPPORTUNITIES CAME FROM SITUATIONS IN WHICH I INITIALLY THOUGHT, 'YOU WANT ME TO DO WHAT?'

Like supervising a team at an assembly plant early in my career, or being asked, as an engineer, to lead Human Resources. That pang of fear you get when you're given a challenging opportunity is a good sign. See it as a motivator and an opportunity to learn new skills, work with new people, and expand your experience."

You don't have to rely on intuition or on "closing your eyes and hoping for the best" to seek, identify, and seize the best learning experiences. You just have to know what to look for.

DIFFERENT EXPERIENCES TEACH DIFFERENT THINGS

Learning experiences fall into distinct categories. Depending on the particular type of experience, different lessons are more likely to emerge. Increases in job scope might improve your ability to handle complexity, make more high-stakes decisions, and manage your work-life balance. A horizontal move might sharpen your political savvy and your ability to look at things from different perspectives. Tackling a turnaround might give you a better understanding of communicating a vision, managing resistance to change, and dealing with ambiguity.

Before you enter any new experience, take a moment to contemplate what the experience is likely to teach you and how that might add to your development. Don't worry that the experience might be difficult or that you might not ever be good at it. Just focus on the potential learning and what you could gain from it.

QUALITY OF EXPERIENCE MATTERS

Some experiences are richer in their potential for yielding significant and lasting learning. Nine components contribute to the developmental value of an experience, including unfamiliar responsibilities, high stakes, influence without authority, and working across cultures. The more of these elements that are present in any one experience, the greater the developmental value or "heat" associated with the experience. These elements will be discussed in greater detail in Chapter 19, "Seeking Experience."

Of course, feeling the heat isn't necessarily appealing. But it's when you're well out of your comfort zone and wondering if you've gotten yourself into more than you can handle that you're actually giving yourself the greatest opportunity to stretch and grow. It may involve some struggle and even setbacks in the short term, but your willingness to embrace the learning experience will lead to significant gains over time.

QUANTITY OF EXPERIENCE MATTERS

The more high-quality learning experiences you acquire, the more potential lessons you can accumulate. Some people are only fortunate enough to have a few standout learning experiences in their careers. The lessons learned from these experiences often serve them well across a variety of circumstances but eventually reach the point of diminishing returns. On the other hand, constantly adding to your stockpile of lessons gives you a seemingly unlimited supply to draw from and apply. Of course, steadily acquiring high-quality learning experiences and continually willing yourself to get out of your comfort zone require some effort.

In addition to the total number of learning experiences you acquire, you also want to consider whether you've accumulated repeated experiences in one of the distinct learning categories. This might seem redundant, but multiple experiences in the same category can add depth and nuance to the lessons you've acquired. Just because experiences occupy the same category doesn't mean they are alike. Just think about the different skills and insights you might acquire from an international assignment in Latin America followed by an international assignment in Southeast Asia.

DIVERSITY OF EXPERIENCE MATTERS

If you've been fortunate enough to acquire a large number of high-quality learning experiences, then the last thing to focus on is making sure those experiences are as varied and distinct as possible. You'll never succeed in "doing it all" but the more diversity in experiences that you encounter, the bigger and broader will be the web of lessons created by these experiences.

COMMON MISUNDERSTANDINGS ABOUT EXPERIENCE

Your ability to grow and develop through your experiences is strengthened by your understanding of the fundamental truths outlined in this chapter. But you can gain even more from your experience if you are also aware of some relevant misunderstandings that can trip you up. Here are three of the most common and important misunderstandings about experience.

MISUNDERSTANDING #1

EXPERIENCE IS WHAT'S ON YOUR RESUME

Thus far, we've only talked about learning and development in the context of experiences that take place on the job. But work isn't the only place where valuable learning can occur. In fact, many individuals who excel at learning from experience will tell you that some of their most valuable lessons learned have come from experiences they've had outside of work.

Just because learning takes place in a setting other than work doesn't mean that the lessons can't be successfully adapted to a work challenge. One individual shared the rather gut-wrenching experience he went through in trying to mediate a family dispute over who should inherit an uncle's property. Through the experience, he learned a lot about dealing with diverse stakeholders under very emotional circumstances in which there was a lot to lose. He later found that the insights and skills he gained from this experience proved quite valuable in negotiating multiparty contracts when interests diverged and emotions ran high.

MISUNDERSTANDING #2

LEARNING ON THE JOB IS MOSTLY ABOUT LEARNING TO DO YOUR JOB MORE EFFECTIVELY

As we mentioned earlier, different on-the-job experiences teach different things. In addition, CCL research shows that the lessons learned from any experience can potentially fall into three different worlds: the World of Work, the World of People, and the World of Self. The lessons that teach us about the self are sometimes the most difficult. They often stem from a particular category of experience we call *hardships*. We'll talk more about those later.

MISUNDERSTANDING #3

LEARNING FROM EXPERIENCE IS AN EVENT

Learning from experience is an ongoing process, not an event. Because of the way that past and present interact, learning from experience never ends. Different perspectives emerge over time. Also, a lesson isn't truly learned until it's applied. Until you can apply the insights you've gained from your previous experiences, their true value lies unrealized.

21

TRUTH #3 — EXPERIENCE IS THE PAST, PRESENT, AND FUTURE AT ONCE

This last truth is a little more abstract than the others but no less important or practical. Your experience isn't limited to the space and time in which it occurred. It has a past, a present, and a future, and the lines between them can blur.

If you appreciate all three of these aspects, you are better positioned to actively leverage your experience and make the most of it rather than just letting it "happen" to you. You also avoid getting stuck in the past, becoming lost in the present, or forever dreaming about the future.

"IF WHAT YOU DID YESTERDAY SEEMS BIG,
YOU HAVEN'T DONE ANYTHING TODAY."
– MIKHAIL GORBACHEV

THE VALUE OF PAST EXPERIENCE IS DYNAMIC, NOT STATIC

Past experience doesn't just get hardwired and have one set of lessons or meanings attached to it. It can be revisited and reflected upon, leading to new insights. Subsequent experiences can bring new perspective to what happened before and cause you to reframe what you've learned. Sometimes an important lesson from an experience lays dormant until an altogether new experience triggers an "aha" that makes you say, "I guess I knew that all along!"

PAST EXPERIENCE AND PRESENT EXPERIENCE ARE IN CONSTANT INTERPLAY

Just as current experiences can cause us to look at the past in a new light, so can past situations add to our understanding of the challenges we encounter today. This dynamic keeps your perspective from becoming rigid and narrow. So try to avoid notions of "keeping the past the past" or "living completely in the moment"—allow the two to mix it up and shape one another.

YOUR FUTURE EXPERIENCE CAN BE SHAPED

You can influence the direction your experience follows, if you so choose. Because much of our learning and development takes place during challenging job assignments, we sometimes overlook our own ability to identify and pursue the experiences that are going to contribute to our growth. Instead, we wait for experiences to come our way (or worse, lay low to avoid them).

Sure, an international assignment isn't something that you can make happen just by walking into your boss's office and asking for it. On the other hand, leading a task force, or volunteering to start up a community of practice, or mentoring a younger colleague are all things that can be made possible without too much back-and-forth.

Once you've identified the general type of experience that will provide you with the right learning opportunities, begin to think strategically about which opportunities you can pursue most quickly and easily. You might be surprised as to how many quality experiences are at your fingertips.

> "I AM ALWAYS DOING THAT WHICH I CANNOT DO,
> IN ORDER THAT I MAY LEARN HOW TO DO IT."
> – PABLO PICASSO

The essence of these truths and misunderstandings is that experience is of immense value to your development as a leader but only if you choose to make the most of it. That is what this book will help you do. Next, we'll introduce you to four fundamental skills that will help you rediscover your past, seize the present, and shape your future.

TRUTH #1

EXPERIENCE MATTERS–LEADERS ARE MADE, NOT BORN
- EXPERIENCE IS THE BEST TEACHER.
- THE VALUE OF EXPERIENCE IS UNIVERSAL.
- YOUR EXPERIENCE IS UNIQUELY YOURS.
- SOME PEOPLE LEARN MORE FROM EXPERIENCE THAN OTHERS.

TRUTH #2

EXPERIENCE IS VARIABLE–NOT ALL EXPERIENCES ARE EQUAL
- DIFFERENT EXPERIENCES TEACH DIFFERENT THINGS.
- QUALITY OF EXPERIENCE MATTERS.
- QUANTITY OF EXPERIENCE MATTERS.
- DIVERSITY OF EXPERIENCE MATTERS.

TRUTH #3

EXPERIENCE IS THE PAST, PRESENT AND FUTURE AT ONCE
- THE VALUE OF PAST EXPERIENCE IS DYNAMIC, NOT STATIC.
- PAST EXPERIENCE AND PRESENT EXPERIENCE ARE IN CONSTANT INTERPLAY.
- YOUR FUTURE EXPERIENCE CAN BE ACTIVELY SHAPED.

LEARN MORE ABOUT
THE LESSONS OF EXPERIENCE

Since CCL first conducted its Lessons of Experience research, it has carried out many follow-up studies to delve further into our understanding of how experience shapes leaders' development. If you'd like to dive deeper into what we've learned, we recommend the following:

McCall, M. W., Jr., Lombardo, M. M., & Morrison, A. M. (1988). *The lessons of experience: How successful executives develop on the job.* Lexington, MA: Lexington Books.

Morrison, A. M., White, R. P., & Van Velsor, E. (1992). *Breaking the glass ceiling: Can women reach the top of America's largest corporations?* Reading, PA: Addison-Wesley.

Van Velsor, E., & Hughes, M. W. (1990). *Gender difference in the development of managers: How women managers learn from experience.* Greensboro, NC: Center for Creative Leadership.

Wilson, M. S. (2010). *Developing tomorrow's leaders today: Insights from corporate India.* Singapore: Wiley Asia.

Wilson, M. S., Van Velsor, E., Chandrasekar, A., & Criswell, C. (2011). *Grooming top leaders: Cultural perspectives from China, India, Singapore, and the United States.* Greensboro, NC: Center for Creative Leadership.

CCL has also published material for human resource executives and others who are looking to approach experience-driven leadership development from an organizational perspective. The following titles offer a number of practical insights and tools from CCL as well as industry and academia:

McCauley, C. D., DeRue, D. S., Yost, P. R., & Taylor S. (Eds.). (2014). *Experience-driven leader development.* San Francisco, CA: John Wiley & Sons.

McCauley, C. D., & McCall, M. W., Jr. (Eds.). (2014). *Using experience to develop leadership talent.* San Francisco, CA: John Wiley & Sons.

Wilson, M. S., & Chandrasekar, N. A. (2014). *Experience explorer: Facilitator's guide set.* Greensboro, NC: Center for Creative Leadership

CHAPTER TWO

THE FOUR ESSENTIAL SKILLS FOR EXPERIENCE-DRIVEN LEADERSHIP

Just as experience is a vast territory, so is leadership. No worries. CCL has studied leadership skills for as long as it has examined the nuances of learning from experience. There are many specific skills, or competencies, that leaders can apply to be successful. But when it comes to making the most of your experience, a few stand out.

That's good, because focus is important when you are trying to develop. Honing in on some core skills, especially if they're complementary or reinforcing, will get you farther faster than taking an "everything under the sun" approach. Don't try to change a dozen things simultaneously. Ambitious and well-meaning as it may be to try to develop everything at once, it simply doesn't work.

The skills we're highlighting are collectively named the *Fundamental Four*.

SELF-AWARENESS   LEARNING AGILITY

COMMUNICATION   INFLUENCE

Note: Each skill has been assigned a color that will be used as a visual reference throughout this book.

Why the *Fundamental Four*? First, they've stood the test of time, and volumes of research reinforce their strong links to leadership effectiveness. Also, they're relevant to leadership at any stage in your career, at any level of the organization where you are a leader, and at any size corporation you may be a part of.

If you are seriously struggling with any one of these four, you may be dealing with the consequences of that at this very moment. On the other hand, if you are one of the few leaders on track to being highly proficient in all four, then you can attest to the many benefits they bring to your performance.

Chances are that among the Fundamental Four, one of them might be less familiar to you than the others. Learning agility is the relative newcomer of the bunch. Although there have been learning agile leaders throughout history, the particular skill itself came into clear focus as a result of the Lessons of Experience study. The actual term *learning agility* wasn't applied until some years later. If this is the first time you've encountered learning agility, then we are excited to introduce you to this intriguing and valuable skill.

As for the other three, you have probably already encountered them several times. We ask you to consider them from a fresh perspective, particularly with respect to how they play a role in making the most of your experience.

Because we're not just going to inform you about these skills but rather guide you in developing them, there are a few other things to note. These are "big" skills; you might call them meta-skills. So to help further focus your development, we're breaking each of them down into four subskills. Also, you can practice and develop the Fundamental Four in all aspects of your life as well as over the course of your entire life. This is especially important because you never truly master these skills but rather are always honing and adding to them with each new experience. And that, of course, is exactly what we hope you do.

So, let's give you a brief introduction to the Fundamental Four.

SELF-AWARENESS

Individuals lacking self-awareness live in a bubble. The bubble protects them from a world that at any moment might challenge and possibly upend the image they've built of themselves. What does this bubble insulate them from? It prevents: criticism, accountability for mistakes, an accurate understanding of both their strengths and limitations. From inside the bubble, the world appears as it should and reflects their underlying beliefs about themselves and others. Life inside the bubble, quite frankly, is pretty good.

GOOD, THAT IS, UNTIL … "POP!" SOMETHING BREAKS THROUGH.

Maybe it's missing a long-sought promotion, getting dropped by a major client, or even getting demoted or let go. Whatever the cause, the bubble is gone and the jolt of self-awareness that occurs can be quite unsettling. If you don't immediately begin trying to reform the bubble, then it can be a moment of profound learning and growth, albeit one that comes at a cost.

It doesn't have to be that way. To some degree, we all form our own bubbles, but self-aware leaders inhabit bubbles that are relatively thin, transparent, and permeable. They're vigilant in keeping them flexible in order to avoid the distressing "pop" that occurs when self-awareness is lacking.

Self-aware leaders approach the world with a degree of confidence similar to their thick-bubbled counterparts, but it's a confidence built of humility and understanding, not of arrogance and self-delusion. Self-aware leaders are confident because they know who they are, why they are, what they are reasonably capable of and not capable of, how their behavior affects others, and how others see them.

Self-awareness doesn't protect them completely from occasional self-inflicted mistakes or flashes of hubris. But they are able to avoid the often-significant peril that comes from overestimating strengths, being blind to major flaws, or completely misjudging their impact on others.

Self-awareness has many facets, but we'll focus on four, given their relevance to making the most of your experiences.

LEADERSHIP WISDOM

You can mine considerable wisdom from your experiences, but, like most mining, some digging is required. We'll give you a variety of useful tools and techniques to help you unearth your experiences and extract the rich insights that inform your understanding of who you are as a leader; insights that you can apply to the leadership challenges that lie ahead.

LEADERSHIP REPUTATION

At one time or another we've all heard the statement, "Your reputation precedes you" directed our way. Depending on the circumstances, our reactions might have ranged from satisfaction and pride to nervousness and embarrassment. We each have a reputation, shaped by others' experiences with us. The objective here isn't to change your reputation but to understand it, both through your own lens and through others' eyes.

30

LEADERSHIP IDENTITY

The American cartoon character Popeye had a signature phrase: "I am what I am, and that's all that I am!" Although it's true that Popeye would have done well to brush up on his influencing skills, we applaud him for his well-developed sense of leadership identity. It suggests that between gobbling cans of spinach and battling his nemesis Bluto, Popeye asked himself a profound question: "What (who) am I?" We'll invite you to do the same. In this particular instance, we'll ask you to frame your understanding of who you are in relation to who and what surrounds you in the present.

LEADERSHIP BRAND

If your reputation is what you have cultivated from your past experiences, then your brand is what you aspire to and what your present-day actions and intentions can support. Creating a brand that is sustainable and serves you well must first be authentic. This requires that you support your actions with a deep and accurate understanding of yourself.

If you currently lack self-awareness, then it may be the most difficult of the Fundamental Four to develop and maintain because the lure of retreating back into a thick, protective bubble can be difficult to resist. It takes some work to maintain a translucent and porous bubble, and life inside can have its uncomfortable moments. But it's far better than the alternative, which is that someday you will hear that dreaded *"Pop!"*

LEARNING AGILITY

Learning agile people are distinguished by their willingness and ability to learn from experience. But they also excel at applying those lessons to perform successfully in new and challenging situations. Put another way, learning agile people have "learned how to learn" from their experiences and have made a strong commitment to seeking new challenges that allow them to apply what they've learned and acquire new lessons for future application.

Learning agility differentiates those who are able to extract the most learning from any given experience and subsequently apply it. Learning agility also makes a difference in career success. Individuals higher in learning agility significantly differ from others on a number of outcomes. Specifically, individuals high in learning agility:

- OUTPERFORM PEERS

- LEARN NEW INFORMATION MORE QUICKLY

- LEARN HOW TO INTERACT MORE EFFECTIVELY

- ADAPT WELL TO WORKING GLOBALLY

- GET PROMOTED MORE FREQUENTLY

- ARE LESS LIKELY TO DERAIL

Over time, bosses and organizations often recognize learning agile people as having high-potential talent. As a result, they receive some of the most sought-after opportunities for leadership and career advancement.

Conversely, people who are less learning agile lack the versatility and adaptability of their more learning agile peers. They are capable of career success but typically within more narrow circumstances that favor a specific set of skills. It's when situations change and new skills and new approaches are required for success that people who are less learning agile encounter difficulties. They tend to cling to what has previously worked for them and don't recognize or heed the signals calling for new skills and new ways of doing things. The more resistant these individuals are to adapting, the higher the probability that they will derail.

CCL's research into learning from experience and the skills of those who excel at it has allowed us to decode the "unconscious competence" of most learning agile people and separate their abilities into four specific sets of behaviors.

SEEKING

Developing learning agility requires an intentional willingness to immerse yourself in new and challenging situations that broaden and expand your experiences. Learning agile leaders see new situations as prime opportunities for new learning and growth. Furthermore, they do more than just accept opportunities that come along. They seek out and embrace these opportunities.

SENSEMAKING

Learning from experience is a highly active and ongoing process marked by curiosity and a willingness to experiment. Asking "Why?" "How?" and "Why not?" are essential to gaining the insight and perspective that fuels learning. Failed experiments, and the setbacks and criticism that accompany them, are just a part of the ongoing journey for learning agile individuals.

INTERNALIZING

Learning doesn't end with the experience. Seeking feedback and taking time to reflect are critical for deepening insight and embedding critical lessons for recall and application. They also strengthen self-awareness, which is essential for dealing with future challenges in a realistic manner and staying open to new learning.

APPLYING

A lesson is not truly learned until it is applied. Learning agile people excel at adaptive learning— accessing principles and rules of thumb from previous experiences and applying them to navigate new and challenging situations. Swiftly adapting to new circumstances based on an understanding of what has (and hasn't) worked in other situations is at the heart of what distinguishes learning agile individuals.

As you've considered the four components of learning agility, you've probably thought to yourself, "That seems pretty basic. So what's the big deal? Isn't that something everyone does on a day-to-day basis?"

Yes and no. The four components do capture the basic pattern and progression of behaviors that inform experiential learning. But the difference is that people who are learning agile engage in these behaviors at a significantly higher level of skill and commitment. And because they are constantly engaged in learning from and applying their experience, they raise that level of skill and commitment on an ongoing basis.

COMMUNICATION

Let's be clear. Communicating as a leader is not merely about delivering your message. Nor is it just about understanding what others have to say. It's a "both-and" proposition. Effective communication occurs when you are *both* conveying your message in an intended manner *and* fully appreciating your audience's response. At the heart of effective communication is an exchange of information that results in shared meaning.

When communication is mishandled, every aspect of leadership becomes more difficult. Misunderstandings occur. Conflicts are either inflamed or left to simmer. Ambiguities remain unresolved. Trust erodes. Thus, leaders who struggle to communicate can find themselves isolated and frustrated with their inability to connect with others and get things done.

These specific communication tools will ensure that you are gathering the most shared meaning from your experiences with others; they represent a balance of being understood and understanding others.

ACTIVE LISTENING

Communication does not consist only of talking and waiting to talk. Engaging in the kind of meaningful dialogue that enriches experience requires you to focus your attention and ask the types of questions that stimulate the expression of others' thoughts and bring out deeper meanings.

GATHERING FEEDBACK

Feedback is a gift. It might not always feel that way, but it's one of the most valuable things you can receive from others. Because all feedback has value, it's important to know how to ask for it, how to interpret it, and how to apply it. When others recognize your willingness to seek and embrace feedback, they're more willing to provide it to you.

DELIVERING FEEDBACK

Delivering feedback to others is just as valuable as receiving feedback. If you want to foster openness and trust in your relationships, model those ideals in the feedback you provide to others. Being specific about the situations you are referring to, the behaviors you observed, and the impacts they had on you will ensure that people receive meaningful feedback messages.

COMMUNICATING YOUR VISION

An idea can't become a reality if it's never put into action, and action can't occur unless the idea is shared. Sharing with others the future you imagine brings clarity to your vision and gathers the energy and support of others. A significant part of that process occurs when you invite others to layer their own ideas and hopes onto yours, creating an inspiring vision shared by everyone.

We communicate all day, every day, so there is plenty of opportunity to practice and develop your skills. Approach your communications with focus and purpose so that you benefit from growing your skills and finding shared meaning.

INFLUENCE

CCL's research defines leadership as a collective social process. The outcomes of this process are direction, alignment, and commitment toward the group's overall goals. Achieving these outcomes is neither easy nor simple. One reason for that is any collective is made up of individuals, all with different needs, values, visions, and agendas.

GETTING THE INDIVIDUALS TO MOVE AS A GROUP IS A CHALLENGE, AND THAT'S WHY LEADERSHIP IS OFTEN LIKENED TO "HERDING CATS."

Harnessing the group's capacity to achieve direction, alignment, and commitment requires leaders to apply a great many skills. One of the most crucial is influence.

All of us make our own decisions and are accountable for our actions. But we don't act in a vacuum; other people are an integral part of the mix. And just as we seek to lead others in a particular direction with particular goals in mind, others are attempting to do the same. That includes bosses, peers, direct reports, customers. There is no organization in which influence is not pervasive and ongoing.

Without the capacity to influence others, your ability to make what you envision a reality remains elusive because, after all, no one can do it alone. Without the ability to capture the hearts, minds, and energy of others, the truly important things in work and in life can't be achieved. These four influence skills will help you stay engaged in achieving direction, alignment, and commitment through your interactions with others.

POLITICAL SAVVY

Just because organizations are supposed to work in an organized and rational manner doesn't mean that's what happens. Far from it. In any organization, other organizations coexist simultaneously: the formal and the informal, the structured and the organic, the spoken and the unspoken. Telling these different organizations apart, understanding where they intersect, and navigating back and forth between them requires political savvy. Otherwise, you can get lost in the maze of experiences you encounter.

SELF-PROMOTION

Everyone you work with is bombarded with information. No matter your role in the organization or how long you've been around, it can be difficult to cut through the clutter. To shake things up and create new possibilities, you need to stand out and get people's attention. That means promoting yourself. The key is to do it authentically and for the right reasons.

BUILDING AND MAINTAINING TRUST

If you don't cultivate and sustain trust with others, then you aren't likely to accomplish significant work. If you're asking others to take risks with you and to choose the path you envision from among alternatives, then you need them to believe in you and your leadership. When trust isn't strong, you may get compliance with your needs but you won't get the commitment that leads to superior results.

LEVERAGING NETWORKS

The model for tomorrow's organization isn't a centralized grid or a series of hubs and spokes. It's a sprawling web that morphs in shape and size. In this dynamic and interconnected world, you need a network of relationships that functions in a similar way. Creating it and knowing when and how to tap into it requires some level of dedication and skill, but your network will be invaluable in generating the types of rich experiences that will fuel your development as a leader.

Despite the worthiness of these four skills, many of us, even long-time leaders, feel hesitant about influencing others, concerned that our actions might be misinterpreted as manipulation. There are two things to say here: First, context matters. Some approaches to influence are more appropriate and effective than others, depending on the situation. Second, you matter. If you are self-aware (as described above) and in touch with your motives and values, you can be confident that you are exercising influence in a responsible way.

Next, Chapter 3 aligns the subskills related to self-awareness, learning agility, communication, and influence with proficiency in rediscovering your past, seizing your present, and shaping your future.

SELF-AWARENESS

- LEADERSHIP WISDOM
- LEADERSHIP REPUTATION
- LEADERSHIP IDENTITY
- LEADERSHIP BRAND

COMMUNICATION

- ACTIVE LISTENING
- GATHERING FEEDBACK
- DELIVERING FEEDBACK
- COMMUNICATING YOUR VISION

LEARNING AGILITY

- SEEKING
- SENSEMAKING
- INTERNALIZING
- APPLYING

INFLUENCE

- POLITICAL SAVVY
- SELF-PROMOTION
- BUILDING AND MAINTAINING TRUST
- LEVERAGING NETWORKS

CHAPTER THREE

APPLYING THE FUNDAMENTALS— THE EXPERIENCE-DRIVEN LEADERSHIP MODEL

The purpose of this book is to give you an enhanced understanding and appreciation of your experience and to provide you with the skills to learn from it and to put those lessons into practice. When we talk about rediscovering your past, seizing your present, and shaping your future, let's be clear about what we're not talking about. With regard to your past, we're not asking you to engage in psychoanalysis or nostalgia. When we talk about the future, we aren't asking you to imagine jetpacks or 3D food printers. And when we talk about the present, we are not talking meditation or daydreaming (although there's nothing wrong with either).

Instead, we're asking you to invest mental and behavioral energy into each of these realms of experience. And we are providing you with specific mindsets, skillsets, and toolsets to maximize your past, present, and future experiences. To avoid getting "stuck" in any of these moments in time, it's best to keep your mental and behavioral energy moving in a fluid and nimble manner, circulating among past, present, and future, pausing briefly when necessary but always focusing on what you need most to lead effectively.

Imagine this flow of energy moving along a continuum that looks something like this.

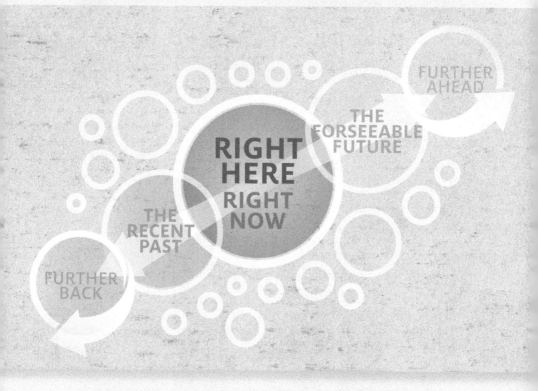

You won't develop the capability to manage that energy overnight. It will seem mechanical at first, and you will need to develop certain skills before you can apply your energy effectively in each of the three areas. But gradually, steadily, you can transform that energy into a reliable, learned set of mental and behavioral practices. As you develop your skillset, the corresponding benefits of experience-driven leadership will become all the more evident.

Now we'll look at rediscovering your past, seizing your present, and shaping your future in the context of the Fundamental Four and the related subskills introduced in Chapter 2. The following graphic provides an overview:

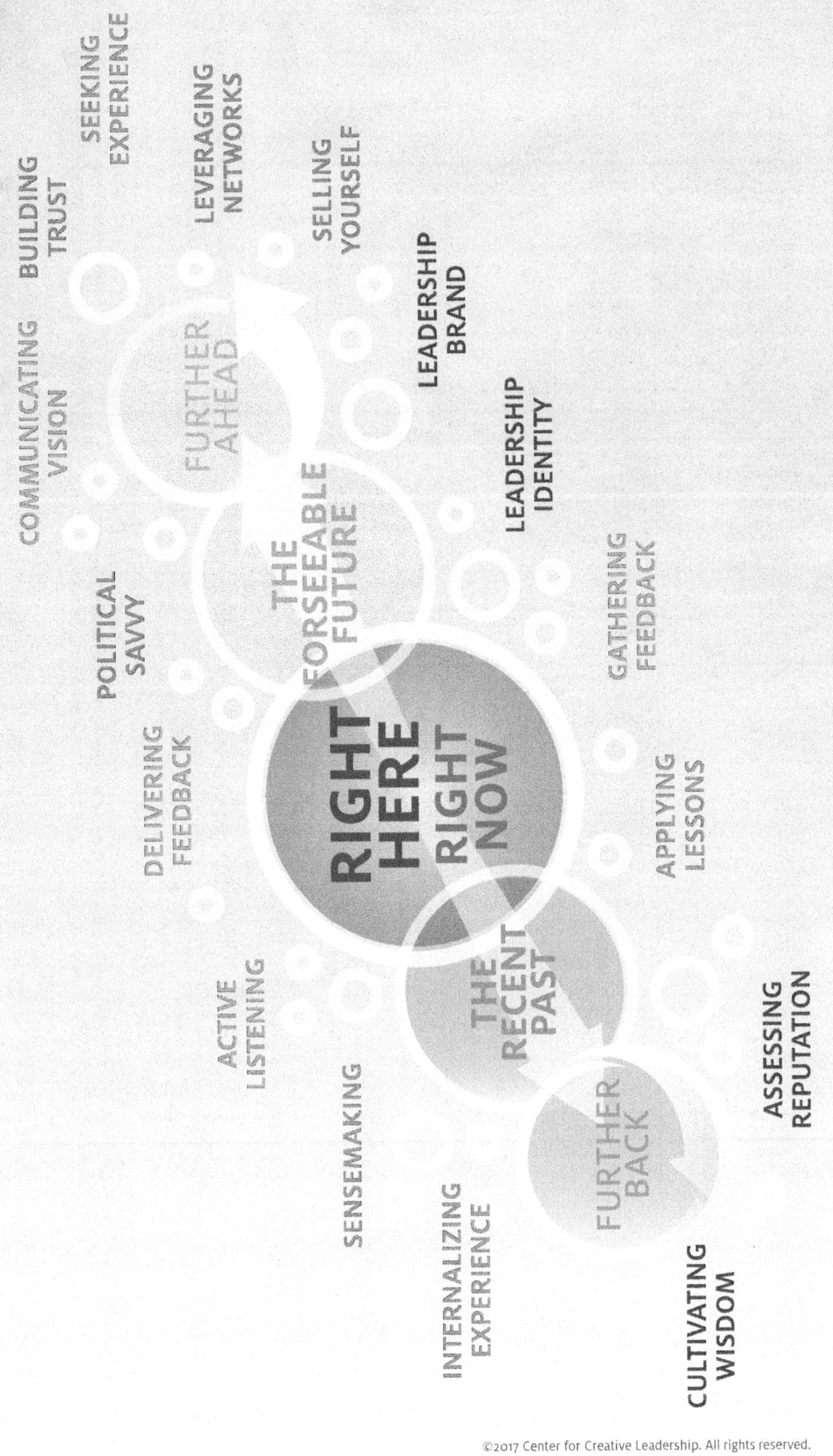

SEEKING EXPERIENCE

BUILDING TRUST

LEVERAGING NETWORKS

COMMUNICATING VISION

SELLING YOURSELF

FURTHER AHEAD

LEADERSHIP BRAND

POLITICAL SAVVY

THE FORSEEABLE FUTURE

LEADERSHIP IDENTITY

DELIVERING FEEDBACK

GATHERING FEEDBACK

RIGHT HERE RIGHT NOW

APPLYING LESSONS

ACTIVE LISTENING

THE RECENT PAST

SENSEMAKING

FURTHER BACK

ASSESSING REPUTATION

INTERNALIZING EXPERIENCE

CULTIVATING WISDOM

43

REDISCOVER YOUR PAST

As American novelist and Nobel Prize winner William Faulkner wrote, "The past is never dead. It's not even past." He's right. The past never really goes away. That may seem unsettling at first, but it's actually a good thing. When you're familiar and engaged with your past and approach it with the right mindset and techniques to understand it, it can reveal any number of things to help inform and drive your journey as a leader. These include triumphs that teach you what you're capable of and mistakes that remind you to avoid certain actions and decisions in the future. Or perhaps your past can bring insights that help you better understand others and how, as a leader, to get the best out of them.

Section II introduces you to a trio of skills that take you beneath the surface of your past experiences so you can appreciate them in a deeper and more vivid manner. Doing so will stimulate the natural interplay between the past and the present. Your understanding and acceptance of your past will also help guide you forward to the experiences that will continue to challenge you and help you grow as a leader.

SEIZE YOUR PRESENT

Are you familiar with the Latin phrase carpe diem? It means "seize the day." But to do that, and do so repeatedly, requires more than a passionate zeal to tackle the challenges you face—it takes skills.

Section III highlights a variety of skills from across the Fundamental Four that help you clearly grasp what's going on around you (even when it appears confusing at first). These skills help you to address present challenges by leveraging your past, to achieve understanding with others, and to understand your place in the organizational maze and how to navigate it.

SHAPE YOUR FUTURE

Thoughts about the future can provoke anxiety. This is a healthy response because it helps keep us prepared and protected from overconfidence. But our vision of the future should also inspire excitement, hope, and a resolve to tackle the challenges ahead. Although there are many more factors at work in the universe than we could ever use to control our future, we can endeavor to shape it.

Section IV breaks down six sought-after leadership skills that help put more of your future in your hands. A common theme is being proactive by stimulating and shaping others' perceptions of your leadership. This helps you create the conditions that lead to direction, alignment, and commitment.

As you put the experience-driven leadership model to work, you don't need to tackle each section in order. Feel free to go where your interests or needs direct you. To help raise your awareness of those needs and assist you in prioritizing your efforts, here is a brief set of questions to consider:

YOUR PAST

- How do your past experiences shape your current approach to leading?

- How often do you take time to reflect on your past experiences?

- Do you gain lasting wisdom from your experiences, or repeat the same lessons over again?

- How aware are you of the reputation you've established as a leader?

- Do you feel your past has lessons to teach that haven't yet been revealed?

YOUR PRESENT

- How do you currently deal with ambiguous situations?

- How often do you apply lessons from your past experiences to new challenges?

- How well are you tuning in to what others are trying to communicate to you?

- How open and transparent are you and others in communicating with each other?

- How effectively do you engage with your broader organization and its "unwritten rules"?

YOUR FUTURE

- What is your vision for how you would like to be seen as a leader?

- How well do you position your skills and accomplishments to others in the organization?

- How strong are the bonds of trust between yourself and key people you rely on?

- How deep and diverse is your organizational network?

- Have you identified future experiences that will help you grow as a leader?

As you work on developing specific skills relevant to your past, present, and future, we encourage you to revisit these questions to see how your answers change.

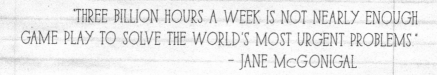

SECTION II
REDISCOVER
YOUR PAST

"THREE BILLION HOURS A WEEK IS NOT NEARLY ENOUGH GAME PLAY TO SOLVE THE WORLD'S MOST URGENT PROBLEMS."
— JANE McGONIGAL

No matter what our parents say, action video games DO prepare us for life in the workplace.

Think about it. Games put the player in a constant state of disruption and risk. They force us to use technologies and platforms that are unproven and ideas that have never been tried. And there is only one means of gaining currency and resources in this game:

TAKE RISKS.

At Ubisoft Sweden, home to the Massive Entertainment development team that helped produce blockbusters "Assassin's Creed" and Tom Clancy's "The Division," that is how the game is played—constant innovation that keeps consumers in a $100 billion industry from getting bored. One of the most cutting-edge innovations has been open-world games, in which control is handed over to the player. That means players need not follow a single, predetermined objective, and there are side missions to explore.

In his approach to the sprawling, 300-employee design floor at Ubisoft, Associate Producer Andre Tiwari fell back on leadership lessons he learned serving 13 years in the U.S. Navy. Rank and title were not the keys to commanding sailors' respect and motivating a crew, and neither was handing out shore leave or pay raises. Similarly, Tiwari noted, designers must have a passion for the journey itself.

"On a fundamental level, both game developers and sailors do what they do because they love it," Tiwari notes.

'NOT FOR MONEY, OR PRESTIGE, BUT FOR THE LOVE OF THE JOB. THAT'S REALLY IMPORTANT BECAUSE IT AFFECTS A LOT OF HOW YOU DEAL WITH PROBLEMS OR MOTIVATION."

Wise leaders know that they need technical expertise and business acumen, and also that they need to be perceived as someone who has something to offer in the form of knowledge, guidance, and support. In order to chart a course and persuade others to follow them voluntarily, these leaders understand that followers must perceive them as delivering value.

The three chapters in this section concern the process of converting past experience into leadership wisdom. Chapter 4 explores the reflective mindset that allows us to derive the full benefit of experience. Chapter 5 deals with the skills by which we internalize successes and setbacks, putting them into perspective as part of a "work in progress." Chapter 6 begins a turn outward, as we gain a picture of how others perceive us as a leader and how we ensure that those perceptions align with our values and desired reputation.

CHAPTER FOUR

CULTIVATING LEADERSHIP WISDOM

What is the difference between knowledge and wisdom?

Most of us have a working definition. Knowledge is the accumulation of facts. Wisdom is what we do with them. It's an acquired ability to synthesize what we know and to distinguish its meaning and importance.

Studies on cognitive psychology and intelligence have unveiled the nature of wisdom and its core elements. Leaders are considered wise when they:

- LEARN FROM EXPERIENCES
- APPLY THE INTELLECTUAL CAPABILITIES NEEDED TO MAKE SOUND JUDGMENTS
- EMBRACE VALUES THAT BENEFIT THEMSELVES AND OTHERS

How we acquire wisdom is no longer a mystery. All leaders stumble upon countless events in their professional and personal lives, but CCL research reveals that only those who learn from their experiences can excel over the long term. There is no way that you can change the past, but it is possible to change your approach to the future by better understanding your past.

In a competitive, fast-changing global economy, which emphasizes not just know-how but innovation and productivity, leaders need to bring as much wisdom as possible to bear on their daily decisions. But therein lies the challenge. Wisdom takes time to develop, and leaders find themselves pulled between making swift decisions and making wise decisions. How do we gain the time it takes to develop wisdom?

It sounds counterintuitive, but one of the ways we help accelerate the learning curve is to pause, step back, and reflect—slow down to speed up. This is how we apply wisdom to today's challenges rather than yesterday's missed opportunities. Improving your capacity to reflect on a variety of experiences—and the broad range of possible responses—develops your capacity to make wise choices.

In critical moments, successful leaders must carefully analyze situations to avoid making serious mistakes.

IN THESE MOMENTS, THE SKILLS OF BUSINESS KNOWLEDGE ONLY GO SO FAR. HOW LEADERS REACH DEEPER, DRAWING ON THE WISDOM OF EXPERIENCE TO SET THE RIGHT COURSE, IS THROUGH REFLECTION.

"KNOWLEDGE COMES, BUT WISDOM LINGERS."
- ALFRED LORD TENNYSON

VOICES OF EXPERIENCE

A CEO WHO SURFS:
SEEING THE WAVE FROM THE SHORE

Testing polymer in the lab is one thing. Catching a wave off Ventura Beach on a reinforced polymer surfboard is another. After spending 27 years building a metals and plastics testing lab for companies from medical to aerospace, Polymer Solutions CEO Jim Rancourt felt his work-drive waning and stepped away for a seven-week sabbatical. First he biked 450 miles along the coast of Maine, learning to cherish the pocket-sized tire repair kit that came in handy when rubber met road and road won. But it was his participation in a week-long brand immersion study with the California company Patagonia that gave him the deepest reflection.

Deliberately getting out of his comfort zone and onto a surfboard, the CEO learned that he had been looking at his business challenges from only one perspective. The difficulty of surfing, when wave after wave is breaking around you, is knowing which wave to catch at precisely the right moment. But when he then stood back on the shore and watched surfers from a distance, it was easy to pick out the best wave and the right moment.

As Rancourt told his employees, the experience changed him because he learned to walk away and see things from a new angle. That required leaving what he called "margins in his day" to leave time for reflection and to prevent frustration.

How might stepping back, seeing things from a new angle, and creating daily space to reflect change your work life and leadership development?

Before we go deeper into how you can cultivate your leadership wisdom, consider the ten behaviors below that typify a wise leader; identify the three that you feel you are currently strongest in and the corresponding three that you feel are most in need of development.

STRENGTH	NEED	
☐	☐	Frequently reflects on his or her experiences.
☐	☐	Pays close attention to his or her thoughts and emotions.
☐	☐	Views reflection as a learning process.
☐	☐	Revisits experiences more than once.
☐	☐	Questions his or her assumptions.
☐	☐	Challenges his or her beliefs.
☐	☐	Takes accountability for his or her mistakes.
☐	☐	Patiently allows wisdom to reveal itself.
☐	☐	Asks open-ended questions that lead to deeper insight.
☐	☐	Contributes to a culture of reflection in the workplace.

Take a moment to reflect on how your perceived strengths and corresponding development needs in this area have played out in the past and currently. As you progress through this chapter, keep in mind how you might augment or leverage these approaches.

THE MINDSET of
CULTIVATING LEADERSHIP WISDOM

CCL's research shows that without the benefit of reflection, more experience does not equal more learning. This continuing research began with McCall, Lombardo, and Morrison's landmark study of leaders in Fortune 500 companies, which was published in 1988. To attain wisdom, it wasn't enough to describe an experience, the study found. Wise leadership entailed reflection:

> "IT IS STAGGERING TO THINK HOW MUCH EXPERIENCE IS WASTED," RESEARCHERS CONCLUDED, "SIMPLY BECAUSE MANAGERS AREN'T ALLOWED OR FORCED TO STOP AND MAKE SENSE OF WHAT HAPPENED."

Done properly and consistently, reflection can shed light on your experience and open a window for future action. In the absence of reflection, experiences can be piecemeal, disconnected, and potentially misleading.

Wisdom is not granted, it is earned. To acquire wisdom, you need to understand that it comes as a result of consistent effort. Becoming wise also requires you to learn from the breadth of your experiences—your successes and your failures—and accept your role in them. Embracing the following realities will help see you through the long journey to wisdom.

THERE IS NO EXPRESS LANE

Leadership wisdom cannot be gained overnight. It takes commitment to regularly check your own behaviors and reflect on your experience. One look is seldom enough. Wisdom often lies beneath the surface, so repeated reflection from different perspectives gradually reveals deeper understanding.

REFLECTION IS NOT PASSIVE

Reflection involves probing, analyzing, synthesizing, and connecting. It is not just thinking about what happened; it is a thoughtful consideration of why things happened as they did and how your experience might be different when viewed from another perspective.

NO PAIN, NO GAIN

Attaining wisdom requires humility, and that means some of our greatest learning comes from mistakes and failures. If we can't come to terms with those events and accept our role in them, the doors to wisdom remain shut. Getting past the pain of our shortcomings can take some time, but only then can we see situations clearly enough to gain the necessary insight.

"EVERY NEW EXPERIENCE BRINGS ITS OWN MATURITY AND A GREATER CLARITY OF VISION."
        - INDIRA GANDHI

THE DEVELOPMENTAL
BENEFITS OF REFLECTION

Reflection is necessary to your leadership development because it:

- GIVES MEANING TO AN EXPERIENCE

- GUIDES CHOICES FOR FURTHER ACTION

- FRAMES AND REFRAMES A PROBLEM OR CHALLENGE

- TESTS YOUR PERSONAL INSIGHTS AND THEORIES ABOUT A PROBLEM OR CHALLENGE

- FACILITATES TRANSFER OF LEARNING TO YOUR OWN CONTEXT AND SITUATION

- HELPS YOU BETTER UNDERSTAND STRENGTHS AND WEAKNESSES

- SURFACES AREAS OF POTENTIAL BIAS OR DISCRIMINATION

- IDENTIFIES POSSIBLE INADEQUACIES OR AREAS FOR IMPROVEMENT

THE SKILLSET of
CULTIVATING LEADERSHIP WISDOM

There are two types of reflection, both of which are important in moving from experience to wisdom.

SURFACE REFLECTION considers behaviors and action.
DEEP REFLECTION considers the assumptions and values that underpin action.

Each type of reflection draws upon different skills. For surface reflection, practice the following:

GET THE LAY OF THE LAND

Surface reflection is helpful because it forces you to think about experiences in a structured way. It encourages you to take a more thorough approach to the problem and prepares you for similar situations in the future. Surface reflection requires you to step back from the experience, think about the actions you took, and see from the perspective of others. Such reflection is important to help you become more aware of your interactions with people and the environment around you.

Surface reflection is important, but it is only the first step. After considering the actions and behaviors taken in a particular experience, you can then consider what led to such behavior. In this way, surface reflection prepares the way for more profound learning.

Deep reflection requires you to identify and challenge your assumptions, imagine and explore alternatives, and apply reflective skepticism. These components of deep reflection will help you become more thoughtful, aware, and deliberate in your choices. Consider the following approaches to deep reflection.

CHALLENGE YOUR ASSUMPTIONS

Deep reflection helps you learn from past experiences and better handle future ones by helping you think about why you see things the way you do, including your experiences. You have certain assumptions about your experiences, and these assumptions shape how you see yourself. Some of your assumptions can keep you trapped in behaviors you want to change. To engage in deep reflection, you first have to be open to the possibility that your passionately held convictions might be wrong, that you may not have all the answers, that there may be other sources of knowledge, views, or ways of seeing that you have not considered.

ASK TOUGH QUESTIONS

It is one thing to derive lessons and insights from experience; it is another thing altogether to see something fresh, to understand it for itself on its own terms. Somewhere in your reflections you may reach moments of decision: Do I choose to be honest about this and its real consequences? Do I want to change? Am I really prepared to face the consequences of change? These become the central questions driving deep reflection.

LEARN BY UNLEARNING

At the heart of this process of reflection is your ability to examine and challenge your habits. It's no easy challenge to unlearn the habits you bring to situations and relationships. It is through your own process of deliberate consciousness, of unlearning, that you can put aside lessons that no longer apply and free yourself from the power that your own past and will can exert on your ability to reflect deeply on experience.

FLIP YOUR SCRIPT

The more you tell yourself or others about who you are and what you do, the more deeply ingrained these stories become in your subconscious. They become the scripts from which you think and act. Being aware of these assumptions is an important step in learning more about yourself. If you revise your vision of yourself to tell about the new behaviors you would like to integrate, then you send a message to yourself and change the script of how you want to be.

BE VULNERABLE

The vulnerability of not having answers and acting in habitual ways has to be faced in deep reflection. Where deep reflection is absent, there is the risk of making poor decisions and bad judgments. Without deep reflection, you may be convinced of your invincibility by your past successes and therefore fail to consider other viewpoints, with possibly serious consequences.

WORD TO THE WISE

Reflection is important in the development of leadership wisdom because it enables you to learn from experience. There are many times when your automatic reactions to events are insufficient to encourage reflection. You should not rely solely on your natural process of reflecting on experience but actively seek ways to ensure that reflection itself becomes a habit, contributing to your continuing development.

With reflection on a variety of experiences, you can develop your capacity to make wise choices. In order to develop wisdom, you must engage with both surface and deep reflection and the habits of reflective practice. Reflection should not be an end in itself. Reflection is connected with the cycle of experience, and you should continue to grow in experience to deepen in reflection.

"MY MENTOR USED TO SAY, WHEN TALKING ABOUT AN UNDERPERFORMER, 'THAT EMPLOYEE DOESN'T HAVE 10 YEARS OF EXPERIENCE— HE HAS TWO YEARS OF EXPERIENCE REPEATED FIVE TIMES.'"
— BILL GARDNER

THE TOOLSET for
CULTIVATING
LEADERSHIP WISDOM:
Reflection Questions

The key to reflection is asking the right questions. Here are some prompts to help you gain insight from your past experiences.

SURFACE REFLECTION

- What was the experience that led to your learning?

- What happened?

- What actions were taken?

- What was the response of others?

- What were the consequences?

- What could or should you have done to make it better?

- What would you do now if you were in a similar situation?

- How can you apply this learning?

DEEP REFLECTION

- What did you learn about yourself through this experience?

- What was good or bad about the experience? Why?

- What are some beliefs that impact the way you view this experience?

- What other knowledge can you bring to the situation?

- What broader issues arise from the situation?

- What seem to be the root causes of the issue or problem addressed?

- What are broader issues that need to be considered if this action is to be successful?

- What might you do differently?

KEY TAKEAWAYS in

CULTIVATING
LEADERSHIP WISDOM

COMMIT TO REGULARLY
PRACTICING REFLECTION.

TAKE AN ACTIVE APPROACH
TO REFLECTION.

EXERCISE HUMILITY IN REFLECTING ON
PAST EXPERIENCES.

REVISIT EXPERIENCES MULTIPLE TIMES
AND FROM DIFFERENT PERSPECTIVES.

ENGAGE IN SURFACE REFLECTION TO
IDENTIFY PAST ACTIONS AND BEHAVIORS.

ENGAGE IN DEEP REFLECTION TO
EXAMINE UNDERLYING BELIEFS AND ASSUMPTIONS.

REALIZE THAT WISDOM IS EARNED
AND TAKES TIME TO ACQUIRE.

CHAPTER FIVE

INTERNALIZING THE LESSONS OF EXPERIENCE

Learning is an ongoing process, not a discrete event. Certainly, learning takes place in the moment and immediately in the wake of an experience. But even when an experience has reached a natural conclusion, memories and impressions remain and the ripple effects of that experience continue. Opportunities for learning never really end.

Gaining insights from experience can be challenging and requires some deliberate effort. Practices such as reflecting, seeking feedback, and embracing criticism take many of us out of our comfort zones, making these practices learning opportunities in and of themselves. Despite the discomfort they can provoke, they are essential to embedding critical lessons for eventual recall and application.

When we do engage in these purposeful acts of awareness-building, the lessons learned fall into three distinct categories, or what we call worlds.

- THE WORLD OF WORK
    (E.G, SKILLS AND PERSPECTIVES TO GET WORK DONE)

- THE WORLD OF PEOPLE
    (E.G, INTERPERSONAL AND SOCIAL SAVVY TO CONNECT WITH PEOPLE)

- THE WORLD OF SELF
    (E.G, MANAGING ONE'S THOUGHTS, EMOTIONS, ACTIONS, AND ATTITUDES)

Some experiences yield more lessons than others, and the proportion that fall into the different categories varies. Some experiences are more challenging to learn from than others. Not because the lessons aren't there to be harvested but because of the negative emotions associated with the experience. These are collectively referred to as *hardship experiences* and fall into the specific categories of mistake, crisis, and career setback.

Hardships are different from the other categories of learning experiences (see Chapter 19 for a full list).

FIRST, most learning comes from the success of meeting a challenge. With hardships, learning often comes from the *lack of success*.

SECOND, though many lessons learned from experience are external in nature (What did I learn about handling my job and working with other people?), lessons learned from hardships are often *internal* (What did I learn about myself?).

THIRD, the lessons learned from hardships often have less to do with the events themselves and more with how you *respond* to them.

People who learn from hardships:

- RESIST BLAMING THE SITUATION OR OTHERS

- CAN STEP BACK FROM THE SITUATION TO GAIN PERSPECTIVE AND RECOGNIZE WHERE THEIR OWN MISTAKES AND SHORTCOMINGS CONTRIBUTED TO THE OUTCOME

- DEMONSTRATE RESILIENCE IN MOVING BEYOND THE PAIN OF THE HARDSHIP EXPERIENCE AND COMMITTING THEMSELVES TO DO SOMETHING ABOUT THE PERSONAL LIMITATIONS THEY HAD REALIZED

Because hardships force people to come face-to-face with themselves, they often experience *a significant shift in their self-awareness* and better appreciate what they can and can't do successfully. People often get *a significant dose of humility* that increases their compassion and sensitivity in dealing with others' mistakes. Finally, surviving the hardship and willing themselves to move forward provides *added strength* to tackle new challenges and face future failures.

Unlike other categories of learning experience, we seldom seek a hardship—hardships find us. But while a hardship experience can be beyond our control, we can control how we respond and how we perceive it (as a failure or as a learning opportunity, for example).

"I'VE MISSED MORE THAN 9000 SHOTS IN MY CAREER.
I'VE LOST ALMOST 300 GAMES. 26 TIMES,
I'VE BEEN TRUSTED TO TAKE THE GAME WINNING SHOT AND MISSED.
I'VE FAILED OVER AND OVER AND OVER AGAIN IN MY LIFE.
AND THAT IS WHY I SUCCEED."
- MICHAEL JORDAN

Before we go further, consider the ten behaviors listed below that typify a leader who excels at internalizing experience and identify the three you feel you are currently strongest in and the corresponding three that are most in need of development.

STRENGTH	NEED	
☐	☐	Seeks candid feedback on his or her performance.
☐	☐	Responds effectively when given feedback.
☐	☐	Takes criticism well.
☐	☐	Embraces his or her past.
☐	☐	Looks back on situations objectively.
☐	☐	Reflects on and learns from a variety of experiences.
☐	☐	Puts setbacks in perspective.
☐	☐	Learns from mistakes.
☐	☐	Bounces back from failure.
☐	☐	Strives for greater self-awareness.

Take a moment to reflect on how your perceived strengths and corresponding development needs in this area have played out in the past and currently. As you progress through this chapter, keep in mind how you might augment or leverage these approaches.

VOICES OF EXPERIENCE

NEIL DEGRASSE TYSON: TURNING CONTROVERSY INTO ENLIGHTENMENT

Pluto isn't a planet. Wait... What?!?

For this planet-shattering news, you can thank (or blame) Neil deGrasse Tyson, Director of the Hayden Planetarium and one of the foremost popularizers of science.

When the story went viral, he found himself at the center of an unexpected controversy. Ironically, there was never any intent on the part of Tyson and his colleagues to kick Pluto out of the roster of planets; rather they just wanted to clarify the categorization of different objects in the solar system. But the press and others understood it differently.

Tyson chose to stand his ground but also approached his critics with a mixture of empathy, humor, and a bit of perspective—this wasn't the first time a planet had been declassified, just the most recent and public incident. He also used the controversy as an opportunity to challenge people to think differently and more broadly about planets as well as the wide variety of other objects that populate our solar system.

How might you take a cue from Tyson's response to the Pluto uproar and navigate your next controversy with insight and grace?

THE MINDSET of
INTERNALIZING THE LESSONS OF EXPERIENCE

Critical to the mindset of those who excel at internalizing is embracing every new experience as an opportunity for new learning and having a deep appreciation for all that experience has to offer them. This "all-in" commitment and intensity allow them to see the learning all the way through, just as Michael Jordan follows through on a jump shot to keep his aim true. To simply move on and let the experience fade would work against gaining the most learning and growth possible. Stopping to linger awhile on what was learned and revisiting and reexamining the experience help to cement the lessons that have already been recognized and to surface new insights. Here are some ways that the learner's commitment and follow through emerge.

MAKE A LOT OF MISTAKES,
BUT DON'T MAKE THE SAME MISTAKE TWICE

Committed learners are comfortable with stumbling their way to success. They distance themselves from the emotional sting, but they keep the memory of their mistakes—and what they learned as a consequence—close at hand. Successfully navigating similar circumstances in the future helps strengthen the takeaways from the original experience.

KNOW THYSELF

Experiences, especially the most difficult ones, have as much impact on self-awareness as the specific knowledge and skills we acquire. Leaders committed to learning from experience value the humility it takes to learn, and they value the insights they gain from experience and integrate them with their existing strengths and limitations. It helps ground them and better prepares them for future challenges because they know what they are and aren't yet capable of doing.

NEVER STOP

Individuals who strive to internalize the lessons of their experience see themselves as continuous works in progress. They yearn to keep growing, to keep getting better. Their learning never ends. There's always something further they can explore and apply to the present, even if it means revisiting their personal past.

MYTH: THOSE WHO EXCEL AT LEARNING FROM EXPERIENCE ARE IMMUNE TO FAILURE.

TRUTH: THEIR TRACK RECORD FREQUENTLY MASKS A LONGER ARC OF SUCCESS AND FAILURE. WHAT DISTINGUISHES THEM (AND FUELS THEIR SUCCESS) IS HOW THEY RESPOND TO FAILURE —WITH RESILIENCE, WISDOM, AND RESOLVE.

THE SKILLSET of
INTERNALIZING THE
LESSONS OF EXPERIENCE

You aren't likely to gather the lessons of experience without pausing to consider just what it is the experience is teaching you. The business world favors action, but remaining mindful and reflective of your experiences will help you build habits from the lessons they offer.

COMMIT TIME TO REFLECT

Monitor your progress and learning. Our hectic, nonstop lives make reflection a difficult habit to form. Make it a part of your routine or put it on your calendar so you can make sure it happens. Record insights in a centralized place (e.g., in a journal or on your smartphone) so you can revisit them later.

REVISIT THE EXPERIENCE

Don't limit your reflection to just reviewing the outcomes—actually replay experiences in your head in as vivid detail as possible to incorporate not just what you did but how you felt as you did it. Also consider others' actions and reactions. As you re-immerse yourself in the experience, record and categorize your insights.

FIND AN "ACCOUNTABILITY PARTNER"

Self-awareness and self-development require an ongoing commitment to a process that will often feel difficult. Just as you can benefit from a workout partner to increase your physical fitness, you may also benefit from a partner who is willing to support, guide, and walk with you on your learning path.

SEEK MEANINGFUL FEEDBACK

Go beyond "How did I do?" and "Give me some feedback." Surface questions will get you surface responses. Ask people you trust to share specific observations about your behavior and how it affected them, and think about what you might do differently in the future.

EMBRACE CRITICISM

Don't frame criticism as right or wrong, good or bad, but as an opportunity for insight and a means to calibrate your future behavior. In order to encourage more feedback, let others know you got the message and appreciate their openness.

PUT SETBACKS IN PERSPECTIVE

Don't run away from mistakes and failures, but don't dwell on them either. Strive to get beyond the pain and disappointment and focus on what can be learned from the experience and applied to future circumstances. Occasionally look back and evaluate the progress you've made.

SEEK EXPERIENCES THAT WILL ENHANCE YOUR SELF-AWARENESS AND CAPACITY TO LEARN

Different experiences yield different insights and lessons. CCL research has identified specific experiences that promote the development of self-awareness and "learning to learn"—see if you can engage in some of these awareness-enhancing experiences:

- TRADE RESPONSIBILITIES WITH A COLLEAGUE AND THEN SERVE AS EACH OTHER'S PEER COACH.

- WORK WITH COLLEAGUES TO REDESIGN A WORK PROCESS.

- ACTIVELY PARTICIPATE IN THE START-UP OF A NEW TEAM.

- TAKE OVER A PROJECT THAT IS IN TROUBLE.

- WORK ON IMPROVING A RELATIONSHIP WITH A DIFFICULT COLLEAGUE.

- WORK IN A SHORT-TERM ASSIGNMENT IN ANOTHER OFFICE/ REGION/COUNTRY.

- TEACH A COURSE INSIDE OR OUTSIDE THE ORGANIZATION.

- LEAD A BENCHMARKING TEAM THAT VISITS AND LEARNS FROM OTHER ORGANIZATIONS.

- PARTICIPATE IN A JOB ROTATION PROGRAM.

- START A NEW GROUP, CLUB, OR TEAM.

- TAKE UP A NEW HOBBY.

"FOLLOW EFFECTIVE ACTION WITH QUIET REFLECTION. FROM THE QUIET REFLECTION WILL COME EVEN MORE EFFECTIVE ACTION."

— PETER DRUCKER

THE TOOLSET for
INTERNALIZING THE
LESSONS OF EXPERIENCE:
Gratitude Journaling

Reflecting means seeing the whole situation—the negative and the positive in fair measure. Of course, it's in our nature to rewind our memory and see only what didn't go right. That indeed serves a purpose, but without a full appreciation of the situation and our role in it, opportunities for learning go untapped.

Focus on the positive and be grateful for the opportunity. Gratitude journaling is a practice that can help us more readily see the positive in situations and ourselves. Before you begin, take a moment to recognize the things in your life that you are always grateful for—loved ones, food, shelter. Set those aside as "givens" on your list.

Now, take a moment at the end of the day to pause for reflection. During that time, identify three things (work-related or otherwise) not on your givens list that you are particularly grateful for and why they made you feel that way.

Consider how that realization makes you see the day and its events in a different light. What else does it reveal?

MYTH: ALL LEARNING IS CONSCIOUS AND METHODICAL.

TRUTH: INDIVIDUALS WHO ACTIVELY REFLECT AND PROBE FOR INSIGHT SOMETIMES SPONTANEOUSLY IDENTIFY LESSONS FROM LONG-AGO EXPERIENCES. IN THE MIDST OF THEIR RELATING A PAST EXPERIENCE, IT'S NOT UNUSUAL TO SEE THE COGNITIVE WHEELS BEGIN TURNING AND AN "AHA!" REALIZATION SURFACES.

KEY TAKEAWAYS in

INTERNALIZING THE LESSONS OF EXPERIENCE

EMBRACE MISTAKES
AND THE LESSONS THAT COME FROM THEM.

TREAT LEARNING AS A CONTINUAL PROCESS.

COMMIT TIME to REFLECTING
ON PAST EXPERIENCE.

REVISIT EXPERIENCES IN VIVID DETAIL.

INVITE FEEDBACK AND
ACCEPT CRITICISM.

PUT SETBACKS IN PERSPECTIVE.

KEEP A JOURNAL TO RECORD REFLECTIONS.

CHAPTER SIX

ASSESSING YOUR LEADERSHIP REPUTATION

Jeff Altheide, the vice president of a public relations agency, once told the story of being introduced to a business executive and telling the executive, "Your reputation precedes you." The businessman, gratified and grinning broadly, inflated his chest and replied, "Thank you!" There was just one problem—the reputation that preceded him wasn't a good one.

When it comes to building a leadership reputation, there are at least two schools of thought. Some leaders see reputation as superficial, subject to distortion, and therefore unimportant. We subscribe to another view: In business, as in life, there is benefit in knowing how other people view you and how you need to improve those perceptions.

We're not suggesting you spin the truth, manipulate your image, or mask who you really are as a leader. Instead, you can make a commitment to recognize aspects of yourself that should be coming across to other people but aren't.

The focus of this chapter is to help you gain a clear picture (unlike the blissfully unaware businessman) of what "reputation precedes you." Later, in Chapter 14 ("Establishing Your Leadership Brand"), we will develop skills to close gaps between what others perceive and what you want to convey. This takes practice and the acquired ability to be comfortable with who you are. But, first, it takes awareness.

> "THE WAY TO GAIN GOOD REPUTATION IS
> TO ENDEAVOR TO BE WHAT YOU DESIRE TO APPEAR."
> – PLATO

Far be it from us to argue with Plato! Your reputation is the perception that others form of you as a result of the impressions you make. The ability to have an impact in the eyes of employees, customers, and other important constituencies affects how well you do your job. That means your reputation can be an asset or a liability.

Reputation is a conduit through which people initially know you. Whether someone is getting to know you through a first meeting, over time, or even through the media, your reputation is being broadcast and formed. In the short term, reputation is important because you have only a few minutes to interact before others draw conclusions about you. In the long term, your reputation is tied to your credibility.

Reputation relates to CCL's approach to leadership as a social process that produces three outcomes (DAC):

- DIRECTION RELATES TO WIDESPREAD AGREEMENT ON THE OVERALL GOALS FOR SHARED WORK.

- ALIGNMENT COORDINATES WORK SO THAT ALL UNDERSTAND, ACCEPT, AND PERFORM THEIR ROLES.

- COMMITMENT ASSUMES MUTUAL RESPONSIBILITY ON THE PART OF THOSE DOING THE WORK.

These leadership outcomes arise from interactions and relationships among people with shared work. The link to reputation is this: How you participate and relate to others defines your reputation, which in turn affects how others interact with you. The way you engage with others in the social process of leadership creates a reputation that others remember and share. So reputation doesn't just precede you. It follows you everywhere you go.

Reputation, although formed in your past, has implications for your present and your future, and at some point, it becomes legacy. If the reputation you have established is at odds with the legacy you envision, you must somehow repair your reputation.

Before we delve further into exploring reputation, consider the ten behaviors listed below that typify a reputation-savvy leader; identify the three that you feel you are currently strongest in and the corresponding three that you feel are most in need of development.

STRENGTH	NEED	
☐	☐	Is aware of his or her reputation.
☐	☐	Understands the impact of his or her reputation on others' current perceptions.
☐	☐	Understands how his or her reputation may affect current or future opportunities.
☐	☐	Regularly re-evaluates his or her reputation.
☐	☐	Examines past behaviors to understand how his or her reputation was formed.
☐	☐	Seeks direct feedback on his or her reputation.
☐	☐	Considers how others might evaluate or react to his or her reputation.
☐	☐	Accepts responsibility for his or her reputation.
☐	☐	Checks alignment of reputation with his or her values.
☐	☐	Checks alignment of reputation with his or her desired brand.

Take a moment to reflect on how your perceived strengths and corresponding development needs in this area have played out in the past and currently. As you progress through this chapter, keep in mind how you might augment or leverage these approaches.

THE LONG SECOND ACT OF SENATOR EDWARD KENNEDY

He was the youngest child of an ambassador to the Court of St. James and grew up in the shadow of three brothers who died young: a pilot and war hero lost on a special mission, an assassinated U.S. president, and a popular presidential candidate likewise assassinated.

Senator Edward "Ted" Kennedy appeared to be the heir to an American dynasty until his reputation was shattered. In 1969 he crashed his car off a bridge in an incident that killed a young female staffer. Kennedy failed to report the accident to police for 12 hours, leaving him under a lingering cloud of suspicion and scandal that permanently dashed his presidential hopes.

How was it, then, that when he died in 2009 of a brain tumor, he was eulogized as the "Lion of the Senate" whose legislative accomplishments in a 47-year career in that body surpassed those of many legendary figures? Though impossibly compromised and continuing to live a public life dogged by tabloid controversy about his private life, Kennedy rebuilt his political reputation by remaining loyal to his constituents, partnering with traditional adversaries, and successfully legislating a social agenda of weight, breadth, and longevity.

Kennedy's biography validates several important concepts about reputation:

1. Personal reputation can help or hurt a career;
2. Professional reputation derives not just from native skill but from the combination of successful interactions with others and the consistent, demonstrated ability to achieve results on matters of substance; and
3. Legacy is a long-term endeavor.

THE MINDSET of the
REPUTATION-MINDED LEADER

Some leaders believe that only what lies ahead is important and that what they did or didn't do in the past, and how others perceived it, shouldn't matter as much. But if you ignore reputation or fail to examine it accurately, you will struggle to lead others. Here are several reasons why you need to focus on understanding and addressing your reputation.

YOU ALREADY HAVE ONE

Is it the reputation you want and need to be an effective leader? By being mindful of your current reputation and taking a proactive approach, you can insure that there is no daylight between how others view you and the reputation you seek. In today's large, geographically dispersed organizations, where employees might only see senior managers in limited contexts, this is more important than ever.

PEOPLE WILL MAKE ASSUMPTIONS ABOUT YOU

In the absence of solid information and frequent communication, people's impressions can be distorted. Erroneous conclusions about who you are as a leader, what you value, and how well you do your job can be damaging to your reputation.

LONG CAREERS DEMAND INVESTMENT

You invest in your career in many ways: education and training, experience, networking, and goal setting. Don't let a negative or poor reputation sabotage your potential. Just as you develop technical expertise and interpersonal skills needed in your job, you should develop your reputation in a way that serves you as a leader.

"YOU CAN'T BUILD A REPUTATION ON WHAT YOU ARE GOING TO DO."
— HENRY FORD

THE SKILLSET for
ASSESSING YOUR LEADERSHIP REPUTATION

Have you ever tried on clothes in front of a three-way mirror that shows a profile of yourself from angles you normally can't see? Surprising but eye-opening. In the same sense, a multi-perspective and clear-eyed look at the reputation you've established with others is essential to understanding how your reputation helps or hinders you. Try these approaches:

REFLECTING AND PROBING FOR INSIGHT

- What three words describe you as a leader? What words would your boss use? What words would your direct reports use? What about other constituencies?

- What feedback have you received about your reputation as a leader? What comments have you heard that may be clues to how others view you?

- What are the reputations of high-performing, well-respected leaders in your organization? How does your reputation measure up? Context matters. Something that contributes to a positive reputation in one organization may detract from it in another.

- Think of a time when your reputation worked to your advantage. How could you replicate that success more often? Think of a time when your reputation didn't serve you well. What could you do differently in the future?

- Consider recent high-profile, high-visibility scenarios you've been involved in: executive team and board sessions, prepared speeches, large groups, product launches. In what situations have you demonstrated behaviors that have either added to or detracted from your reputation?

GENERATING MORE INSIGHT

Insight is a great way to learn more about how people see you and what they take to be your reputation. Here are some suggestions for how to go about gathering insight.

SEEK FEEDBACK

Talk to people in your organization to get a better handle on your reputation. With some people, the direct approach will work; with others it is wise to look for clues and ask indirectly. Find out if your organization uses 360-degree assessments.

FIND A FOCUS

Pick one aspect of your reputation and focus on it for just one week. What do you notice about yourself? What do you do that supports the reputation you want to have? What is limiting or undermining you? Enlist a coworker to observe you for the week and to give you feedback on your progress.

SIT IN THE HOT SEAT

One component of CCL's Leadership at the Peak program simulates a media interview on a business talk show. Try this with your communications or human resources department. Have an interviewer ask about your vision for a current project, as well as problems and successes. Record yourself and critique the segment with a group of trusted colleagues or friends. How do you come across? Is this how others perceive you and thus contributes to your reputation?

"IT TAKES 20 YEARS TO BUILD A REPUTATION AND FIVE MINUTES TO RUIN IT. IF YOU THINK ABOUT THAT, YOU'LL DO THINGS DIFFERENTLY."
– WARREN BUFFET

THE TOOLSET for
ASSESSING YOUR
LEADERSHIP REPUTATION:
Reputation-Values-Brand Alignment

The following exercise helps you evaluate whether your current reputation is aligned with your values and what you want to be known for. Start by defining your current strengths as viewed by yourself and others. Next, define your development opportunities from your own perspective and that of others. Consider the gaps between the two, and answer the following questions:

- What is your current role and how long have you been in this role?
- How strong is your knowledge and skill level in this role? What would others say?
- In your current role what are you doing very well?
- What areas do you want to improve? Is this about knowledge or skill or something else?
- How would people describe you, and why?
- How would you describe yourself, and why?
- What do others' descriptions suggest about your values? Do they match your assessment?
- Where are the gaps? Why do you think they exist?
- Are you satisfied with your ability to reach your personal and career goals?
- On a scale of 1 to 10 (with 1 = "not satisfied at all" and 10 = "completely satisfied") how would you rate your reputation?

KEY TAKEAWAYS in

ASSESSING YOUR LEADERSHIP REPUTATION

DON'T IGNORE your REPUTATION
—IT MATTERS!

UNDERSTAND the IMPLICATIONS
OF YOUR CURRENT REPUTATION.

CONSIDER THE ROLE OF YOUR REPUTATION
IN YOUR LONG-TERM CAREER SUCCESS.

ASK PROBING QUESTIONS
TO EXAMINE THE REPUTATION YOU'VE ESTABLISHED.

SEEK FEEDBACK ON YOUR REPUTATION.

MAKE NOTE OF YOUR BEHAVIOR
SO YOU CAN SEE YOUR ACTIONS AS OTHERS DO.

CHECK ALIGNMENT OF YOUR REPUTATION
WITH YOUR VALUES AND YOUR DESIRED BRAND.

SECTION III
SEIZE YOUR PRESENT

When Michelle Wigmore received a call ordering her elite Wild Mountain firefighting unit to deploy by sunrise to the oil boom town of Fort McMurray, this was hardly the Alberta unit's first foray into danger. But the 16 wildfires that comprised the fire that came to be known as "The Beast" created a multi-threat environmental disaster for Canada, burning out of control for six weeks in 2016. Lethal enough was the usual heat, oxygen, and fuel, with higher than normal temperatures, wind, and forests surrounding the "wild-urban interface."

Even worse, as the fires raced northward, was an alarming new risk: If firefighters could not hold the line, the fires would reach Alberta's tar sands. Though the sands themselves are not flammable, the vapors and storage tanks of volatile chemicals surrounding them are highly combustible and would be hard to extinguish. As the scale of the disaster became clear, firefighters looked to experienced leaders like Wigmore to lead them through the job alive. She was known for demonstrating mastery under pressure, making wise decisions, and leading from a forward position by doing the heavy lifting.

Based on Wigmore's reputation, firefighter Kristian Toivonen left a position leading another crew to be Wigmore's subleader.

"I LIKED THE INDIVIDUAL," HE SAID. "I LIKED HER PERSONALITY, I LIKED HER LEADERSHIP, AND HER COMPETENCY, MORE THAN ANYTHING."

WILD FIRE

Arriving at Fort McMurray, the 20-person unit and their leader's ability to coordinate, communicate, and keep cool  were immediately put to the test as firefighters battled flames reaching a thousand degrees Celsius. In one of their first days deployed, the firefighters worked 24 hours straight in an attempt to keep the fire from reaching the airport. The firefighters kept losing, but Wigmore also kept them alive. As Branden Aasman, another firefighter on the team, described it, "She just makes sure that safety is No. 1, and that we're always in a good place. Our safety is never compromised with her."

As firefighters can attest, learning happens in real time, and wise leadership enables trust and contributes to the ability of an organization to work effectively. In this section, we turn to making sense in the moment and applying the lessons of experience, and we offer a research-tested recipe for engaging your leadership style.

Chapter 7 examines how we make sense of experience in the moment through a mindset of adventure. We focus on the skills of constant questioning and adjusting. Chapter 8 walks us through how we can apply lessons (a process that constitutes true learning) through flexible thinking across situational contexts, intuitively finding "Aha!" moments via analogies and connections.

Chapters 9 through 13 are step-by-step resources for developing and applying leadership skills in the present: How we learn and practice active listening, how we gather and deliver real-time feedback, how we understand the role identity plays in the workplace (both ours and others), and how we develop, demonstrate, and leverage political savvy to accomplish personal and organization goals without compromising our integrity.

7

SENSEMAKING—
LEARNING IN THE MOMENT

At one time or another, most of us have heard this timeless wisdom from someone coaching us on an underutilized or dormant skill:

"IT'S JUST LIKE RIDING A BICYCLE."

Such a reassuring thought. No matter how rusty we might be in the performance of a skill, once we get started, something equal to muscle memory will engage and the whole operation will come naturally and effortlessly.

There's just one assumption, of course:

WE LEARNED TO RIDE A BICYCLE IN THE FIRST PLACE.

If this is indeed true, think back to what the experience of learning to ride a bike was like.

Probably, it was combination of things. At the outset we were motivated and determined to try, because the possibilities of speed and mobility were clearly worth any scraped knees. Next, naturally, we fell down and scraped our knees. Then we got up and pondered our mistakes. Gradually, through repeated efforts, we got a handle on the basics. We had to keep the bicycle moving forward, watch where we were going, not make sharp turns, use the brakes and maybe enlist someone to run alongside us with a steadying hand until we found our balance.

So what happened along the journey from tumbling over our handlebars to coasting along on two wheels?

Consciously or not, we made sense out of the experience, gaining not just a new skill but also insight into our capacity to improve and make things happen.

WHAT WE'LL CALL SENSEMAKING IS A KEY PROCESS IN CULTIVATING EXPERIENCE-BASED WISDOM, BECAUSE LEARNING IS SOMETHING WE ACTIVELY SEEK, AND SOMETHING THAT BUILDS ON ITSELF.

Having rediscovered our past in the previous unit, let's now take a closer look at the active and immersive process we use to gain real-time insight into our development. Before we unpack the contents of the mindset, skillset, and toolset involved in sensemaking, a quick self-assessment will provide a personal baseline.

Consider the following behaviors that typify a leader who excels at sensemaking. Of the ten behaviors, identify the three that you feel you are currently strongest in and the corresponding three that you feel are most in need of development.

STRENGTH	NEED	
☐	☐	Makes midcourse corrections.
☐	☐	Tries new approaches.
☐	☐	Is open to others' perspectives.
☐	☐	Acknowledges lack of expertise on an issue.
☐	☐	Tolerates ambiguity or uncertainty.
☐	☐	Learns through trial-and-error.
☐	☐	Readily asks questions.
☐	☐	Persists through missteps and failures.
☐	☐	Challenges the status quo.
☐	☐	Immerses self in new learning opportunities.

Take a moment to reflect on how your perceived strengths and corresponding development needs in this area have played out in the past and currently. As you progress through this chapter, keep in mind how you might augment or leverage these approaches.

"WITHOUT EXPERIMENTATION, A WILLINGNESS TO ASK QUESTIONS AND TRY NEW THINGS, WE SHALL SURELY BECOME STATIC, REPETITIVE, AND MORIBUND."
– ANTHONY BOURDAIN

MINDSET of the
SENSEMAKING LEADER

We've established that successful leaders are made, not born. Successful leaders develop by learning from their experiences. So how do people open themselves to what a learning experience has to offer?

BE A TRAVELER, NOT A TOURIST

A traveler doesn't visit new places as a spectator but becomes immersed in the experience and opens oneself to the possibility of being changed by it. Seeking adventure as an everyday mindset (rather than a holiday from what we do the majority of the time) is a different way of engaging the world. It opens the door to surprise, inspiration, and innovation.

You don't necessarily need to travel far in order to see things differently. A journalist we once knew advised novice reporters to venture outside their routines (and their comfort zones) in search of news. Covering new ground applied to life at work and outside work, she observed.

TAKE A DIFFERENT WAY TO GET TO THE OFFICE. TALK TO THE PERSON IN LINE BEHIND YOU AT THE BANK, AND THE TELLER WHO WAITS ON YOU, TOO. TRY A NEW SANDWICH PLACE AT LUNCH. LISTEN TO A DIFFERENT RADIO STATION. IF YOU ONLY GO PLACES YOU KNOW, AND ONLY TALK TO THE CIRCLE OF PEOPLE YOU ARE COMFORTABLE WITH, HOW WILL YOU LEARN ANYTHING NEW?

VOICES OF EXPERIENCE

RIDHIKA PIRAMAL:
UNPACKING THE "GOOD OLD SUITCASE"

What happens when the Indian economy is opened to the world, and your family's revered, name-brand luggage threatens to get lost in a multinational onslaught of frequent flyers like Samsonite? For Radhika Piramal, who in 2010 became managing director of her father's company, VIP Industries, the world's second largest luggage brand, it was time to reimagine and transform.

Knowing that the good old days of a 70 percent market share were unsustainable, Piramal studied the needs of young travelers and repositioned the flagship line. First came the launch of lightweight, brightly colored polycarbonate luggage with four wheels for easy mobility. With the emphasis on style and agility, the company used TV spots featuring youthful Bollywood stars chasing down city streets in Europe. The new Skybags became the fastest growing brand in India.

But even with a new line for business travelers, Piramal's instinct told her that "long haul" luggage, the traditional purview of her father's company, was too limited, because travelers don't buy luggage that often. The more frequent purchases were backpacks and other day bags designed for the office, with features like laptop protection and comfortable shoulder straps. Moreover, there was money to be made in women's designer bags. Connecting these factors drove the thinking behind the Caprese division, using trends from Milan. For VIP's product development, it was about thinking outside the "good old suitcase," and about being quick to spot trends and react to them.

"WE HAVE TRANSFORMED OUR PRODUCTS ACROSS ALL BRANDS," PIRAMAL SAID, "GETTING THE RIGHT PRODUCT TO THE MARKET."

Piramal didn't approach her problem passively or tentatively. She took it straight on and delved beneath the surface for insight, shifting her perspective and shifting her actions as new aspects of the problem came to light.

How might Piramal's situation and her approach to sensemaking inform how you address urgent threats your business is currently facing?

BEING A NOVICE

Like a new reporter learning where to look for stories, and like Piramal's effort to think outside established parameters, you can also approach the world with the curiosity and fresh perspective of a traveler to a new destination. There is language to learn, culture to understand, a different currency to figure out. Nothing is assumed or taken for granted, and sometimes you will get things wrong.

Adopting a beginner's mindset requires humility and acceptance of a degree of uncertainty. It's like arriving at the airport in a new city.

We might board the wrong bus. We might lack the exact fare. We might get lost. But that's all part of the journey, and sooner or later, we will get where we are going—often with a memorable story to tell. Rather than set out to demonstrate our knowledge and competency, or seek to confirm our preconceptions, we instead reveal our aptitude for embracing the unexpected. The novice mindset is to observe, ask questions, engage in playful experimentation, and be interested in the answers. Novices might just as easily say, "I've never done this before but why not give it a try?"

THE SKILLSET That
"MAKES SENSE"

ANTICIPATE LEARNING

Vigilant sensemaking requires mental preparedness. Say you have
an opportunity to embark on a new experience—an international
assignment, rotation into a different role, or working on an
interdepartmental team. Envision the possibilities by asking yourself

WHAT NEW CHALLENGES AM I FACING?

WHAT MIGHT I LEARN FROM THEM?

WHICH PAST EXPERIENCES MIGHT BE USEFUL TO ME?

EXPLOIT AMBIGUITY

Creativity requires freedom to find new approaches. Situations without
rigid instructions—or perhaps no instruction manual at all—are the very
situations that give us room to invent. Rather than feeling inhibited by
the absence of a problem with a clear solution, we can actually feel liberated
to define the question on our own terms and seek an answer that suits
our needs.

"LOOK AT SITUATIONS FROM ALL ANGLES,
AND YOU WILL BECOME MORE OPEN."
- DALAI LAMA

MYTH: PEOPLE WHO ARE AGILE LEARNERS EXCEL AT EVERYTHING.

TRUTH: AGILE LEARNERS ARE GENERALISTS MORE SO THAN EXPERTS, AND TEND TO BE VERSATILE AND ADAPTABLE.

SWITCH LENSES

Ever tried on a pair of eyeglasses that belongs to someone else? Disorienting, isn't it? But in a sense, this is similar to what effective leaders do when sizing up a problem. They look at it through multiple lenses— for example, that of an employee, a customer, a supplier, a competitor. These leaders make themselves comfortable with the disorientation. Gradually, the blurriness subsides and a clear picture emerges. They also apply different "lens coatings," such as cultural or disciplinary (for instance, management, marketing, or engineering). Today's challenges seldom reveal themselves in a single glance and often have multiple layers. Successfully addressing these problems requires us to change the way we look at them.

GET STARTED

So what now? We anticipated the learning potential of the challenge, accepted its ambiguity, and sized it up from various perspectives. The next step is to dive in, which is sometimes the best way to see what works and settle on a strategy. Rapid prototyping is one way to do that. Begin with a pilot project and execute small-scale experiments that help you develop clarity and confidence. Test your theory in real time, and if the experiment fails, fail fast and make adjustments as you go.

"IF YOU ARE BUILDING A HOUSE AND A NAIL BREAKS,
DO YOU STOP BUILDING OR DO YOU CHANGE THE NAIL?"
- RWANDAN PROVERB

QUESTION YOURSELF AND OTHERS

While making sense of a situation, we often experience a running, in-process dialogue with our teammates and ourselves. What is important here? What are we sensing and feeling? What do our instincts and gut reactions tell us? These aren't yes-or-no questions designed to get facts or force snap judgments. Underlying this constant questioning is a search for new approaches to everyday problems. A few techniques can help us practice this skill.

- TRY SOMETHING NEW. Repeating the same process and the same way of doing things doesn't leave room for new possibilities. Be intentionally experimental and monitor what works and what doesn't. Resist the inertia of old routines or of falling into new routines.

- QUESTION TRADITION. Conventional thinking—"That's the way we've always done it"—is not always the most efficient or effective way to solve problems. It's just the most firmly entrenched. There could be a better way, and it could be eminently doable. But it can only happen if someone is willing to rethink the status quo.

- REINVENT. Experiment and note the outcome. Sometimes an alternate approach, especially when we lack resources, yields an optimum outcome. Some of the most important discoveries come about by accident.

99

> **MYTH:** SUCCESSFUL PEOPLE DO WELL AT EVERYTHING THEY TRY.
>
> **TRUTH:** WHAT DISTINGUISHES SUCCESSFUL PEOPLE IS HOW THEY RESPOND TO FAILURE WITH RESILIENCE, PERSISTENCE, AND WISDOM.

PREPARE YOUR MIND AND BODY FOR LEARNING

When entering a new situation, be mindful of your own outlook and reactions, staying in tune and not losing control. Here are some approaches to try.

TAKE A DEEP BREATH.

Slow, deep, conscious breathing for just five or ten minutes a day supports the ability to concentrate and stay focused, even in stressful situations.

BE POSITIVE.

Negative outlooks can inhibit efforts to work toward creative solutions. Staying optimistic and highlighting the hopeful and even humorous side fosters collaboration.

PRACTICE HUMILITY.

Taking work seriously doesn't mean you have to take yourself too seriously. Showing humility and vulnerability can ease the awkwardness, frustration, and pain of learning situations.

LAUGH.

An occasional laugh cuts the tension others may be experiencing, reduces stress, and promotes resiliency. And the burst of oxygen that laughter requires is good for the brain!

THE TOOLSET for
SENSEMAKING:
Probing Questions

Effective leaders are curious about new situations, and express this by asking probing questions. Their questions are neither random nor superficial but designed to penetrate the surface problem and get at the root causes. When encountering a new and challenging situation, use probing questions to generate insight. One model of questions we call "The Three Ps."

PURPOSE: "WHY DO WE . . . ?"

PRACTICES: "HOW DO WE . . . ?"

POSSIBILITIES: "WHAT IF WE . . . ?"

The Three Ps aren't limited to one round. Keep forming and reforming these questions until you arrive at the essence of the problem and begin to generate promising solutions.

KEY TAKEAWAYS in

MAKING SENSE OF EXPERIENCE

- BE AN ADVENTURER.
- ANTICIPATE CHALLENGES.
- USE DIFFERENT LENSES.
- EXPLOIT AMBIGUITY.
- DIVE IN AND MAKE ADJUSTMENTS.
- QUESTION YOURSELF AND OTHERS DURING THE PROCESS.
- PRACTICE HUMILITY
  -DON'T FORGET TO LAUGH.

CHAPTER EIGHT 8

APPLYING THE LESSONS OF EXPERIENCE

We talked in Chapter 5 about focusing on the thinking and behaviors that help us capture the lessons of experience. But looking inward is only half of the process. A lesson isn't truly learned until it has been applied outwardly.

If we never tapped the knowledge and insights gained from experience, our world wouldn't really change. The challenges we face would persist. We wouldn't change much either. Our growth as leaders would stagnate. Applying the lessons of experience marks that crucial shift that occurs when we put learning into action. It's what allows us to say, "I am now different because . . . ."

Because applying involves the adaptation of past learning to a new challenge, it requires a mixture of flexibility, creativity, and intuition. It is challenging and sometimes frustrating, but it can also yield exciting "Aha!" moments and well-earned accomplishments.

Experience-driven leaders believe that constant curiosity eventually pays off. There's no such thing as "useless trivia" or "random events" in their worlds. They recognize that steadily gathering knowledge and insight helps stimulate more and more connections in their awareness and understanding of new situations.

The interconnected thinking and fluid actions that typify leaders who excel at applying are the product of a diverse set of behaviors. Of the ten behaviors listed below, identify the three that you feel you are currently strongest in and the three that you feel are most in need of development.

STRENGTH	NEED	
☐	☐	Acts on his or her insights.
☐	☐	Seeks inspiration from diverse sources.
☐	☐	Separates what's familiar from what's new in a problem.
☐	☐	Continually searches for new solutions.
☐	☐	Evaluates progress based on what he or she has learned.
☐	☐	Starts over after setbacks.
☐	☐	Adjusts to changes in circumstances.
☐	☐	Applies lessons from experience to new challenges.
☐	☐	Trusts intuition when solutions to problems are not clear.
☐	☐	Forms novel associations and ideas that create new and different ways of solving problems.

Take a moment to reflect on how your perceived strengths and corresponding development needs in this area have played out in the past and currently. As you progress through this chapter, keep in mind how you might augment or leverage these approaches.

VOICES OF EXPERIENCE

EDDIE VEDDER AND THE
"HANDS-ON" LESSON OF THE UKULELE

Eddie Vedder is known as the frontman of Pearl Jam and one of
the prominent voices of modern rock, but part of his songwriting
inspiration comes from a small, seemingly unlikely source: the ukulele.

While traveling in Hawaii, Vedder spotted a lone ukulele for sale in
a cluttered drugstore window and bought it on a whim. Waiting for a
friend across the street, Vedder sat down on some stacked cases of
beer, and by the time his friend appeared, Vedder was halfway through
the first of many songs he would pluck out on the tiny instrument.

Little did he realize that the ukulele would become not only an
enjoyable diversion but also a handy tool for sketching out melodies
and rethinking his work.

"My hands were on it. But it just taught me so much that changed
the way I wrote songs," he told a Boston newspaper. "Whether anybody
was going to hear these songs or not, it was assisting me and furthering
whatever direction I had as far as writing songs for the group."

He added, "I was able to apply ukulele to whatever I'm trying to
write. It's become part of songwriting for me, the knowledge I gained
from hearing the melodies come out, and then applying that to guitar
or vocals."

The simple act of trying something new led Vedder to grow
in an unanticipated direction. By transforming his insights into
action, he was able to capitalize on the parallels and connections
between his experiments with the ukulele and his larger, more complex
compositions for Pearl Jam.

How might you seize upon an unexpected or overlooked source
of insight to bring about a fresh approach to solving a problem that
matters to you?

THE MINDSET of
APPLYING EXPERIENCE

Flexible thinkers like Vedder avoid looking at the world in finite, categorical terms. They favor a more fluid mindset where boundaries blur and shift and where categories might be established only to be reshaped based on new information. Typical notions such as beginning and ending, success and failure, should and shouldn't inhibit our ability to generate and apply solutions.

Here are some ways that "boundary-less" thinking emerges.

(ENDLESS) POSSIBILITIES

A solution always exists. It just hasn't been discovered yet. This keeps us in searching mode and considering "What if we . . . ?" and "How might we . . . ?" versus "We didn't" or "We can't" conclusions. This also helps us build off each other's ideas with the use of "Yes, and" responses.

IT'S ALL RELATIVE

Nothing is ever as new as it seems. Whether it's our own experience or someone else's, there's a connection to something that has happened before.

AM I GETTING BETTER?

Goals are important, but the drive to improve supersedes the desire to achieve. A steady focus on making progress and strengthening one's approach overshadows concerns about how far away the eventual goal is.

"MANY OF LIFE'S FAILURES ARE PEOPLE WHO DID NOT REALIZE HOW CLOSE THEY WERE TO SUCCESS WHEN THEY GAVE UP."
- THOMAS EDISON

THE SKILLSET of
APPLYING EXPERIENCE

A lesson is not truly learned until it is applied. Experience-driven leaders excel at adaptive learning: accessing principles and rules of thumb from previous experiences and applying them to navigate new and challenging situations. Adapting to new circumstances based on an understanding of what has (and hasn't) worked in other situations is at the heart of the lessons of experience. The strength of experience-driven leaders is that they combine their ability to learn from experience with an ability to apply what they have learned. Put another way, the experience-driven leader has "learned how to learn."

ACTIVELY SEARCH FOR PARALLELS AND CONNECTIONS
In new situations, you don't have direct experiences to guide you. Instead, reference indirect or even seemingly unrelated experiences. What about them might be applicable to the current challenge you are facing? You never know what analogies might exist and what solutions might emerge.

FOCUS ON THE FAMILIAR
When facing a new challenge, it's easy to get overwhelmed by all that is different about it. Instead, focus on what you've done in the past that is somehow like the current experience. What helped you in those situations that might apply to the current one? One experience-driven leader referred to this practice as "improvising from a base of strength."

TRUST YOUR INTUITION
New and challenging experiences are characterized by ambiguity. When problems themselves aren't clear, neither are the solutions. Relax the need to come up with "the" answer and trust your instincts to guide you toward "an" answer to start you down the path to better insight and better solutions.

"TRUST YOUR INSTINCT TO THE END, THOUGH YOU CAN RENDER NO REASON."
- RALPH WALDO EMERSON

MYTH: PROBLEMS HAVE "BEST" SOLUTIONS.

TRUTH: PROBLEMS HAVE "BETTER" SOLUTIONS. FROM THE PERSPECTIVE OF AN EXPERIENCE-DRIVEN LEADER, "BEST" SOLUTIONS, TO THE EXTENT THEY EVEN EXIST, ARE TEMPORARY IN NATURE. SINCE MOST OF THE PROBLEMS THEY ENCOUNTER ARE FUZZILY DEFINED, HOW CAN THERE BE CERTAINTY REGARDING THE SOLUTIONS? FURTHERMORE, WHEN THE PROBLEM IS DYNAMIC IN NATURE AND CONSTANTLY EVOLVING, SO MUST THE PURSUIT OF A SOLUTION. FOR EXPERIENCE-DRIVEN LEADERS, STRIVING FOR CONTINUOUS IMPROVEMENT AND FRESH INSIGHT TRIUMPHS OVER ESTABLISHING "BEST" PRACTICES.

CARRY ON

In unfamiliar circumstances, first solutions rarely work. Sometimes second, third, and fourth solutions don't either. Persevere and remain resourceful to generate alternative approaches and gain insight from each attempt. Focus on the learning that occurs, not the frustration. Grit and tenacity will get you through!

BUILD YOUR OWN BRAND OF RESOURCEFULNESS

Everyone is different. Look at what's unique about you and how you approach hurdles. Over? Under? Around? Through? Over time, your signature style will start to emerge.

"PERSEVERANCE IS FAILING 19 TIMES AND SUCCEEDING THE 20TH."
- JULIE ANDREWS

MASH IT UP

If you are without a solution, explore unlikely combinations to stimulate new insights. Don't be afraid to be a little ridiculous or unrealistic. Do a "cocktail napkin" sketch of what this new solution might look like and see what thinking it inspires in others. Then see what new perspective you might have gained on the challenge you're facing.

STIMULATE YOUR SENSES

Sometimes we think about problems and solutions in overly literal terms and get fixated. Find inspiration and reinvigorate your imagination by temporarily shifting your attention to metaphorical representations of the challenge you are facing. Images, films, stories, music, even smells—all can unlock something in your awareness to give you a new perspective and the ability to generate fresh solutions.

MEASURE LEARNING AND PROGRESS

Addressing new and challenging problems is typically a long journey. Frustration comes easily when you are only measuring yourself against the eventual outcome you are seeking. Instead, focus on the progress you've made from the beginning and what you've learned. Having and recognizing a few "early wins" is beneficial to navigating the long road ahead.

MYTH: INSIGHTS "REVEAL" THEMSELVES.

TRUTH: INSIGHTS NEED TO BE COAXED OUT OF THE SITUATION. BEYOND JUST SORTING OUT WHAT HAPPENED AND WHY IT DIDN'T WORK, EXPERIENCE-DRIVEN LEADERS RE-THINK THE PROBLEM TO SEE WHAT THEY CAN LEARN FROM THEIR EFFORTS, INCLUDING WHAT THEY ARE LEARNING ABOUT THEMSELVES.

VOICES OF EXPERIENCE

SHOE LEATHER: THE BUSINESS FOOTING OF NATASHA BARBER

What on earth do IT, strategy, innovation, finance, and children's motor-skill development have in common? One answer is the career of Natasha Barber, an Australian entrepreneur who applied her academic and IT leadership skills to create SKEANIE Shoes for Kids, an online store whose product line has achieved global reach.

Barber, today a design-industry thought leader, was trained in financial services and began her career running her own IT management projects, then opened a brokerage. Becoming a new mother opened her entrepreneur's eyes to a gap in Australia's clothing market: the kind of affordably-priced, quality leather shoes she had bought for her baby in Denmark.

This was the inspiration for SKEANIE, which allowed Barber to apply her background in web development, management, and finance to e-commerce. The result of her hybrid skillset— academic, business, and leadership—was a multilayered approach that integrated Barber's philosophy across departments, so that operations, sales, and marketing functioned seamlessly.

"To be a successful business owner, you need to be courteous but also conscious of employees and have a long-term vision," said Barber, whose company also supplies 160 stores in Europe, Singapore, and the United States. "I have always been a big believer in wrapping yourself up with people who help inspire change, create a movement, and make you to be the best person (both business and professionally) you can be."

Following Barber's example, how might you draw from the diverse experiences of your past and the inspiration of those around you to create entirely new solutions?

THE TOOLSET FOR
APPLYING EXPERIENCE
Making the Most of the Here and Now

The toolset for applying the lessons of experience also incorporates some of the insights from Chapter 7. Though we've presented sensemaking and applying as separate skills, they often occur simultaneously and reinforce one another. The end result is a special combination of meaning-making and behavior that is all about being in the moment and taking fluid action as you wrestle with an immediate challenge.

The questions below draw off the curious notions that fuel both sensemaking and applying and unite them into an integrated approach to inquiry that allows you to embrace a current learning situation to its fullest.

MYTH: LEADERS MUST CLIMB EVERY MOUNTAIN.

TRUTH: THERE ARE LIMITS TO WHAT THEY CAN DO, AND THESE LIMITS ARE HUMBLING BUT NOT DISCOURAGING. EXPERIENCE-DRIVEN LEADERS ADOPT A LONG-TERM VIEW AND RECOGNIZE THEY'VE MADE A CONTRIBUTION TO MEETING THE CHALLENGE THAT OTHERS WILL SOMEDAY COMPLETE.

MAKING THE MOST OF
THE HERE AND NOW

How am I feeling about this challenge?
How is that affecting my behavior?

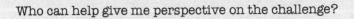

How are others feeling/behaving?

Who can help give me perspective on the challenge?

How can I approach this with a beginner's mindset?

How might I frame it differently?

How can I probe for more insight? ("Why...?" "How...?" "What if...?")

How might I go about experimenting with solutions?

How am I making progress? What am I learning as I go?

What is my intuition telling me?

What does this situation remind me of?

What experiences in my past might inform my approach
to this challenge?

KEY TAKEAWAYS in

APPLYING THE
LESSONS OF EXPERIENCE

THINK FLEXIBLY.

STRIVE FOR CONTINUOUS IMPROVEMENT.

SEARCH FOR CONNECTIONS
AND ANALOGIES.

TRUST INTUITION.

PRACTICE PERSEVERANCE
AND RESOURCEFULNESS.

EXPLORE UNLIKELY COMBINATIONS.

TAP UNLIKELY SOURCES OF INSPIRATION.

CHAPTER NINE

ENGAGING IN ACTIVE LISTENING

Hearing is not the same as listening. Every moment of every day, if we're blessed with healthy ears, there are sounds. Sounds surround us to the extent that we routinely tune them out—traffic, the hum of a refrigerator, conversations in a café.

Only when something out of the routine occurs do you listen to these sounds. Two cars collide in traffic. The refrigerator suddenly stops humming. A café patron at the next table mentions the name of your company. Now you're not just hearing. You are listening with attention, gathering information, assessing the meaning of what you're hearing.

Active listening occurs when we make a conscious effort. It is a selective, critical activity that we practice at a deeper level than hearing. The trouble is, most of us receive little or no training in listening. That's not the only barrier. Assessments of thousands of leaders who have studied with CCL indicate that many of them need to develop their listening skills. Some of what they should improve includes

- DEALING COMFORTABLY WITH PEOPLE'S FEELINGS
- ACCEPTING CRITICISM WELL
- TRYING TO UNDERSTAND WHAT OTHERS ARE THINKING BEFORE MAKING JUDGMENTS
- ENCOURAGING DIRECT REPORTS TO SHARE
- USING FEEDBACK TO MAKE NECESSARY CHANGES IN THEIR BEHAVIOR
- BEING OPEN TO THE INPUT OF OTHERS
- TRYING TO ADOPT SOMEONE'S PERSPECTIVE AND IMAGINE THEIR POINT OF VIEW

Poor listening has a far-reaching impact. Colleagues, direct reports, and others often describe poor listeners in these ways:

- HE ONLY LISTENS TO CERTAIN PEOPLE.

- SHE'S ALREADY MADE UP HER MIND. WHY DOES SHE BOTHER TO ASK WHAT WE THINK?

- HE'S NOT REALLY INTERESTED IN WHAT I HAVE TO SAY.

- SHE'S ARROGANT.

- HE DOESN'T PAY ATTENTION TO WHAT'S GOING ON UNDER THE SURFACE.

- SHE'S JUST REALLY HARD TO TALK TO.

- HE'S VERY CRITICAL OF EVERYONE. NO ONE WANTS TO SPEAK UP ONLY TO BE CRITICIZED.

- I CAN'T GET THROUGH A SENTENCE WITHOUT HER INTERRUPTING.

Active listening makes a huge difference in our interactions with others, fostering trust, respect, and mutual understanding. How can you truly say you are "in the moment" and taking in all that an experience has to offer if your only way of understanding and interpreting that experience comes from yourself? To truly take it all in, you need to gather insight and perspectives other than your own. Active listening is essential to merging your understanding with others and gaining a more complete and integrated understanding of what you, and others, are experiencing together.

LISTENING TRAPS!: EXTERNAL PRESSURES

A volatile, uncertain, complex, and ambiguous environment makes it tempting not to listen. The daily demands placed on leaders make it difficult to slow down, focus, inquire, and listen. At the same time, a critical skill for dealing with uncertain conditions is actively soliciting information and making sense of it. Communicating effectively—especially the ability to listen well—is a survival skill.

Active listening is not optional or a nicety to make others feel good. It is essential to addressing the challenges facing today's leaders. Consider the ten behaviors listed below. Identify the three that you feel you are currently strongest in and the corresponding three that you feel are most in need of development.

STRENGTH	NEED	
☐	☐	Makes people feel they are truly heard.
☐	☐	Shows a willingness to listen and be open to input.
☐	☐	Pays attention to others' nonverbal communication.
☐	☐	Demonstrates empathy toward others.
☐	☐	Listens patiently.
☐	☐	Listens without judgment.
☐	☐	Reflects back to others what they are thinking and feeling.
☐	☐	Asks clarifying questions.
☐	☐	Restates key points.
☐	☐	Understands others before sharing own perspective.

Take a moment to reflect on how your perceived strengths and corresponding development needs in this area have played out in the past and currently. As you progress through this chapter, keep in mind how you might augment or leverage these approaches.

CONNECTING: WHAT IF OPRAH WINFREY WERE YOUR BOSS?

Everyone knows that Oprah Winfrey is one of the most successful and influential TV interviewers of all time, much of this due to her listening ability. But how does her on-air interpersonal skill carry over to her style as a manager?

Consider a job interview she conducted with a candidate for a production opening a few years back. After the initial conversations, it came time for the candidate to negotiate his salary. Each time Winfrey's team named a figure, the interviewee came back with a higher figure. This went on for five rounds of negotiation. Finally the candidate came back with an exorbitant figure far above the going rate.

Winfrey stopped the negotiation and asked a question: "What do you really want?"

The candidate replied, "I want you to want me at your company as much as I want to be there." She assured him that she did, and they returned to negotiating a reasonable salary.

What was her takeaway?

"I realized," Winfrey later wrote, "he was saying the same thing we're all saying to the people in our lives. 'I want to know that you value me.'"

How can you incorporate lessons from Winfrey's interviewing style—connection, empathy, summarizing back what you have heard and understood—into your own interactions?

Think of the bosses you've had and their comparative willingness and ability to hear and understand. Chances are, you have a good sense of what active listening looks like. However, you may not know what to do to be successful at it. Learning and committing to the mindset and behaviors of active listening can improve your ability to both listen and lead.

THE MINDSET of
ACTIVE LISTENING

The quality of conversation improves when you practice active listening. Leaders who practice active listening draw out more information and more meaningful information during a conversation. When practiced with consistent skill, it establishes the norm for conversation and everyone involved is a full participant. Conversations are characterized by finding common ground, connecting to each other, and opening up to new possibilities.

The two key mindsets that drive active listening are to approach listening as an opportunity for learning and to withhold judgment. Actively listening is not just waiting for our turn to speak, and this needs to be clearly demonstrated. So we'll highlight not only what you need to be thinking on the inside but showing on the outside.

LISTENING AS LEARNING
-THINK IT!

A primary goal of active listening is setting a comfortable tone and allowing time and opportunity for the other person to think and speak. To get in the frame of mind of a listener and a learner, focus on the following:

- BE PRESENT AND FOCUSED ON THE MOMENT. ELIMINATE UNNECESSARY DISTRACTIONS.

- REMEMBER THAT YOUR INTENTION IS TO CONNECT TO AND UNDERSTAND-NOT INTERROGATE.

- OPERATE FROM A PLACE OF RESPECT, LETTING YOURSELF EMPATHIZE WITH THE OTHER PERSON.

- BE COMFORTABLE BEING SILENT.

- REMEMBER THAT YOU'LL NEED TO SUMMARIZE THE OTHER PERSON'S IDEAS. PREPARE TO DO SO.

LISTENING AS LEARNING
-SHOW IT!

You can say as much with your body language as you do with the words you speak. When engaged in active listening, your actions go a long way toward communicating your intent to understand.

CONVEY THE APPROPRIATE NONVERBAL COMMUNICATION
Maintain comfortable eye contact. Show interest. Lean forward. Keep your body language open. Give nonverbal affirmations. Nod when you understand. Smile when appropriate. Keep the other person talking.

RESPOND TO THE OTHER PERSON'S NONVERBAL COMMUNICATION
Pay close attention to the other person's nonverbal behavior in order to pick up important information and make sense of it. Look for cues and shifts such as tone of voice, intensity, volume, facial expressions, and posture. By focusing on the other person and being present, you convey that your purpose is to learn.

EMPATHIZE
Put yourself in the other person's place, to temporarily live in that person's world. Demonstrating empathy expresses your willingness to understand the other person's situation and to respect his or her views and experiences. Some examples:

- "I'D BE EXCITED, TOO, IF I HAD SUCH ATTRACTIVE OPTIONS BEFORE ME."

- "IT MUST BE REALLY HARD TO MAKE THIS CHOICE."

- "THAT EXPERIENCE MUST HAVE REALLY TESTED YOUR DETERMINATION."

"I REMIND MYSELF EVERY DAY:
NOTHING I SAY THIS DAY IS GOING TO TEACH ME ANYTHING.
SO IF I'M GOING TO LEARN, I MUST DO IT BY LISTENING."
- LARRY KING

WITHHOLDING JUDGMENT–THINK IT!

As a listener and a leader, you need to be open to new ideas, perspectives, and possibilities. Even when good listeners have strong views, they suspend judgment, hold their criticism, and avoid arguing or selling their point of view right away. Tell yourself, "I'm here to understand how the other person sees the world. It is not time to judge or give my view."

Holding judgment is particularly important when tensions run high. To maintain a judgment-free mindset in these situations, focus on the following:

- LET THE OTHER SIDE VENT OR BLOW OFF STEAM IF NEEDED.

- DON'T FEEL COMPELLED TO JUMP IMMEDIATELY TO PROBLEM SOLVING OR OFFERING ADVICE.

- BE COMFORTABLE NOT TALKING; YOUR JOB IS TO PAY ATTENTION AND UNDERSTAND.

WITHHOLDING JUDGMENT—
SHOW IT!

ACKNOWLEDGE DIFFERENCE

Each person brings a unique perspective to a situation. Experience, culture, personal background, and current circumstances all contribute to the way people react at work. Communicate that you'd like to understand things through the other person's point of view.

INDICATE YOUR OPEN MIND

Show your genuine intention to be open-minded by saying things such as:

- "I'M COMING FROM ANOTHER PERSPECTIVE AND I WANT TO UNDERSTAND YOUR VIEW."

- "MY GOAL HERE IS TO UNDERSTAND, NOT TO JUDGE OR MAKE A DECISION."

- "I REALLY WANT TO UNDERSTAND WHAT IT IS THAT YOU'RE THINKING AND FEELING."

BE PATIENT

Allow the other person to talk and elaborate. Allow pauses. Don't speed the conversation along.

THE SKILLSET of
ACTIVE LISTENING

Demonstrate that you are tracking with the information being presented by periodically restating the other's basic ideas, emphasizing the facts. This act of paraphrasing allows you to identify any disconnects and signal to the other person that you are getting it.

PARAPHRASE TO REFLECT

Like a mirror, we can reflect information and emotions without agreeing or disagreeing. Use paraphrasing—a brief, periodic recap of the other person's key points—to confirm your understanding of what they've told you. Don't assume that you understand correctly or that the other person knows you get it. Paraphrasing facts helps identify any disconnects and signals to the other person that you understand. Use responses such as:

- "WHAT I'M HEARING IS . . ."

- "LET ME MAKE SURE I UNDERSTAND WHAT YOU'RE SAYING . . ."

- "IF I'M UNDERSTANDING YOU CORRECTLY . . ."

PARAPHRASING EMOTION

This is an important aspect of the active listening skillset but challenging to put into practice. The emotional message may be in the words used, the tone, body language, or some combination. Using this technique shows the other person that you are expending attention and energy to understand what he or she is communicating. This might also help others articulate unconscious feelings. Here are some examples.

- "YOU SEEM TO HAVE DOUBTS ABOUT . . . "

- "IT SEEMS TO ME THAT YOU ARE FEELING VERY HAPPY ABOUT . . . "

- "SOUNDS AS IF YOU'RE FEELING PRETTY FRUSTRATED AND STUCK."

ASK OPEN-ENDED AND CLARIFYING QUESTIONS

Double-check any issue that is ambiguous or unclear. Open-ended questions (as opposed to yes-or-no questions) draw people out and encourage them to expand their ideas. They also encourage people to reflect, rather than justifying or defending a position or trying to guess the "right answer." Examples are:

- "WHAT ARE YOUR THOUGHTS?"

- "WHAT LED YOU TO DRAW THIS CONCLUSION?"

- "WHAT WOULD HAPPEN NEXT?"

CLARIFYING QUESTIONS help clear up confusion. They define problems, uncover gaps in information, and encourage accuracy and precision. For example:

- "LET ME SEE IF I'M CLEAR. ARE YOU TALKING ABOUT . . . ?"

- "I MUST HAVE MISSED SOMETHING. COULD YOU REPEAT THAT?"

- "I AM NOT SURE THAT I GOT WHAT YOU WERE SAYING. CAN YOU EXPLAIN IT AGAIN ANOTHER WAY?"

ASK PROBING QUESTIONS

New ideas or suggestions can be introduced into a conversation not only by making statements but also by asking well-formulated questions. Probing questions invite reflection and a thoughtful response rather than dictate a solution. This helps develop problem-solving capacity in others. For example:

- "MORE SPECIFICALLY, WHAT ARE SOME OF THE THINGS YOU'VE TRIED? CAN YOU GIVE ME A FOR-INSTANCE?"

- "HOW DIRECT HAVE YOU BEEN WITH MARCUS ABOUT THE CONSEQUENCES FOR THE SALES FORCE IF THE SITUATION DOESN'T CHANGE?"

- "WHAT IS IT IN YOUR OWN LEADERSHIP APPROACH THAT MIGHT BE CONTRIBUTING TO TONYA'S FAILURE TO MEET HER DEADLINES?"

"THERE IS ONE CARDINAL RULE.
ONE MUST ALWAYS LISTEN TO THE PATIENT."
- OLIVER SACKS

RESTATE TO SUMMARIZE

Briefly recap core themes raised in the conversation. Summarizing helps people see their key ideas, and it confirms and solidifies your grasp of them. It may lead to additional questions and clarify mutual responsibilities and follow-up. Briefly summarize what you have understood as you listened with comments such as:

- "IT SOUNDS AS IF YOUR MAIN CONCERN IS . . ."

- "THESE SEEM TO BE THE KEY POINTS YOU HAVE EXPRESSED . . ."

You can also ask the other person to summarize:

- "WHAT HAVE YOU HEARD SO FAR?"

- "TO MAKE SURE WE'RE ON THE SAME PAGE, WHAT ARE THE KEY PLANS WE'VE AGREED UPON TODAY?"

SHARE YOUR PERSPECTIVE

Being an active listener doesn't mean being a sponge, passively soaking up the information. You are an active party to the conversation with your own thoughts and feelings. Yet active listening is first about understanding the other person, then about being understood. That's hard to learn and apply, especially for leaders accustomed to believing that they must get their message out so that others can follow.

As you gain a clearer understanding of the other person's perspective, introduce your ideas, feelings, and suggestions and then collaborate on next steps. For example:

- "YOUR TELLING ME ABOUT THIS INCIDENT TRIGGERED A THOUGHT."

- "I FELT SO HAPPY TO HEAR THAT I WASN'T THE ONLY ONE FEELING THAT WAY."

- "MAY I SHARE SOMETHING SIMILAR?"

LISTENING TRAPS!: TIME AND PLACE

Listening is particularly challenging when you aren't in the same room with others involved in the conversation. In telephone calls and video conferences, nonverbal cues are missing, technology may be distracting, and the lure of multitasking is strong. The reality of routinely working across time zones and with coworkers anywhere in the world makes active listening all the more important.

THE TOOLSET for
ACTIVE LISTENING:
Create Reminders

Developing active listening skills requires steady practice. Unfortunately, we seldom take sufficient advantage of practice opportunities, so we suggest making a reminder list of your own and finding ways to position it to capture your attention when the things on your list are most needed.

For example, try

- TAPING A LIST TO YOUR COMPUTER OR ABOVE YOUR DOOR SO YOU CAN GLANCE AT IT WHEN OTHERS ENTER THE ROOM

- TUCKING YOUR LIST INTO YOUR WALLET OR KEEPING IT WITH YOUR NOTEBOOK OR SMARTPHONE

- KEEPING IT SIMPLE AND JUST WRITING "LISTEN" AT THE TOP OF YOUR NOTES AT EACH MEETING

If you are working on a more specific skill, give yourself a cue.

- INTERRUPTING TOO MUCH? KEEP A CARD HANDY THAT SAYS "DON'T INTERRUPT!"

- HONE YOUR QUESTIONING SKILLS? REFER TO A CONVENIENT LIST OF OPEN-ENDED, CLARIFYING, AND PROBING QUESTIONS.

- JUST AS YOU THINK THROUGH THE CONTENT OF THE MEETING IN ADVANCE, THINK THROUGH YOUR LISTENING STRATEGY. MAP GOALS, BEHAVIORS, AND QUESTIONS TO REMIND YOU AS THE MEETING UNFOLDS.

KEY TAKEAWAYS in

ENGAGING IN
ACTIVE LISTENING

- LISTEN TO LEARN

- ESTABLISH A JUDGMENT-FREE ZONE

- PARAPHRASE INFORMATION AND EMOTION

- ASK OPEN-ENDED, PROBING, AND CLARIFYING QUESTIONS

- RESTATE KEY THEMES

- SHARE YOUR OWN THOUGHTS AND FEELINGS

- CREATE LISTENING REMINDERS

CHAPTER TEN

GATHERING
ONGOING FEEDBACK

There is an old newsroom joke about the grizzled city editor's suggestion box that takes various forms, depending on who tells the joke.

In one version, the box is nailed to the wall but has no "in" slot. In another variation, the box has a slot but no bottom—and it hangs over a trash can. Either telling has the same terse message:

"NO FEEDBACK WANTED."

This chapter advances the opposite idea, with strategies for experience-driven leaders to identify who can give them valuable feedback, when to create conditions for gathering that feedback, and how to receive it. Whereas we've talked previously about the value of interpreting past events, this is about the benefits of using feedback as a method for interpreting events in real time.

131

If you're a manager who has just completed a leadership development experience, such as attending a program or receiving feedback from a 360-degree instrument, or have just experienced a career transition, such as a promotion or a lateral move to a more challenging position, these strategies can help. The same is true if you currently find yourself struggling or have recently experienced a career setback.

DON'T: Seek feedback from your fan club only.

DO: Respect those who do not wish to give you feedback.

How does gathering feedback work? Feedback provides information that lets you know how you are doing. If you are monitoring your everyday work, it lets you know how you measure up. If you have set a development goal for yourself, it reinforces the changes you are making, boosts self-confidence, and encourages you to continue. In a new job, it lets you know whether you are learning the skills required. If you are experiencing difficulties, it helps you evaluate your progress.

IVAN LENDL: PUTTING THE BALL IN ANDY MURRAY'S COURT

Numbers don't lie. But for tennis champion Andy Murray, they didn't tell the whole story.

Coming into 2016 many thought Murray the best player in the world. But that's not what the rankings said. He had lost multiple Grand Slam finals, falling short of his goal to topple Novak Djokovic as No. 1. But in the summer, Murray began his ascent to the top, winning the critically important Wimbledon title for the second time in his career.

Both those wins had something in common: Coach Ivan Lendl was in Murray's corner. The retired Czech player, a former champion who struggled to realize his potential, traveled a similar career path. He was able to give Murray authentic, honest, even blunt assessments—counsel Murray referred to as "home truths."

Murray didn't need someone to teach him tennis or how to reach the upper echelon. Because competitive finals often hinge on one or two points out of five hours of play, he needed the toughness to prevail. In that regard, Lendl was steely-eyed and disciplined, a coach but not a friend. He advised Murray to eliminate distractions, withdraw from social media, avoid court outbursts, and focus mentally and physically on one objective: winning.

"Ivan's very solid," Murray told reporters. "He'll never lie to you, and it's not always easy to find someone like that."

What can the coach-player relationship between Lendl and Murray teach you about gathering ongoing feedback in terms of identifying who is capable of giving it, when to ask for it, and how to receive it?

WINNER

Whether you're trying to win a major sporting event or integrate a new acquisition, ongoing feedback helps you make the most of your present experiences. It's crucial for calibrating your behaviors in the moment:

STOP, START, CONTINUE, DO MORE, DO LESS, DO IT DIFFERENTLY.

Accurate, timely feedback engages leadership behaviors that create direction, alignment, and commitment when things aren't working or have gone too far in one direction.

But you can't reap these benefits if you don't ask for feedback. Nor is it enough just to get the feedback. How you react to it and decide to act (or not act) on it sends a critical signal to others. Sending the right signals will encourage others to give you proactive feedback.

DON'T: Ask the person to defend his or her opinion (there is a difference between "defending" and "explaining"). Feedback is purely subjective perceptions and information. You can place your own value on it later.

DO: Ask clarifying questions, and explain how you would like to receive your feedback. **Example:** "Rachel, can you picture that event in your mind and describe where we were, what I did, and how you felt about it?"

Take a moment to evaluate the ten behaviors listed below and identify the three you feel you are currently strongest in and the corresponding three that are most in need of development.

STRENGTH	NEED	
☐	☐	Seeks candid feedback on his or her performance.
☐	☐	Seeks feedback from a variety of people.
☐	☐	Seeks feedback in a timely manner.
☐	☐	Seeks feedback on specific behaviors and their impact.
☐	☐	Asks questions to clarify and better understand feedback.
☐	☐	Is not afraid to ask others about his or her impact on them.
☐	☐	Is not threatened by criticism.
☐	☐	Is easy to give feedback to on his or her performance.
☐	☐	Responds effectively when given feedback.
☐	☐	Accepts criticism well.

Take a moment to reflect on how your perceived strengths and corresponding development needs in this area have played out in the past and currently. As you progress through this chapter, keep in mind how you might augment or leverage these approaches.

THE SKILLSET of
GATHERING
ONGOING FEEDBACK

Feedback provides information that lets you know how you are doing. If you are monitoring your everyday work, it lets you know how you measure up. If you have set a development goal for yourself, it reinforces the changes you are making, boosts self-confidence, and encourages you to continue. If you are in a new job, it lets you know whether you are learning the new skills that are required. If you have experienced a career setback, it gives you information that helps you evaluate the situation.

Many people know that they need feedback but are unsure about how to get it. Three things must be considered: **who to ask, when to ask,** and **how to ask.**

ASK THE RIGHT PEOPLE

It should be someone

- whose opinion you respect and who will encourage you to improve your effectiveness, someone with credibility and integrity. Ask yourself: "Is this someone I trust to be honest with me, who does not have a hidden agenda, and who treats me with respect?"

- who has a different work style and whose feedback will provide opinions and points of view that are new. Someone who will help move you outside your comfort zone.

- with whom you must interact in order for you both to be successful. This is a relationship where each of you has a vested interest in making the other person work more effectively.

- with whom you have worked long enough to have had opportunities to observe you in a variety of settings. This usually means at least six months.

Overall, you need people who

- are able to observe your behavior
- have an interest in your effectiveness
- are able to speak to you directly, honestly, and specifically

Fortunately, such people exist in all aspects of your day-to-day life, and aren't limited to coworkers.

ASK AT THE RIGHT TIME

Identify your focus areas for development. Otherwise, asking for feedback will be difficult and you risk using up your coworkers' goodwill because it's unclear what you want. The more often you receive feedback, the more often you can put your goals into action.

ASK THE RIGHT WAY

Asking for feedback is difficult. The quality and quantity of the information that you receive is influenced by how you ask for it. Try CCL's **Situation-Behavior-Impact (SBI)** method for eliciting relevant feedback. The SBI approach provides others with a specific, helpful framework for structuring their information and perceptions of you.

SITUATION.

Where and when did the specific behavior occur?
("In our staff meeting this morning, when we were meeting with Grace.")

BEHAVIOR.

What are the characteristics, actions, verbal and nonverbal behaviors that were observed?
("You criticized Grace's idea before it was explained, and revealed through your body language that you didn't think much of it.")

IMPACT.

What are the consequences of the observed behavior on others?
("Grace's idea had merit and you didn't hear it through. Your behavior also inhibited the other people there.")

DON'T: Interrupt the other person.
You asked for the feedback, now listen to it.

DO: Allow for pauses, and let the person finish what he or she is saying. Then try to paraphrase either back to the person or in your own mind.

ASK FOR FEEDBACK OFTEN

Practice makes perfect. Seek feedback on a daily basis if you can, so that it is not out of the ordinary. Practice also makes permanent. Seeking and receiving feedback will become easier to do, will be welcomed by others, and will be rewarding professionally and personally.

> "UNHAPPY CUSTOMERS ARE ALWAYS A CONCERN.
> THEY'RE ALSO YOUR GREATEST OPPORTUNITY."
> - BILL GATES

THE MINDSET of GATHERING ONGOING FEEDBACK

Now that you have received the feedback, let's focus on what to do with it. Unlike the gruff city editor who placed the suggestion box over the waiting trash can, the assumption here is that someone motivated to ask for real-time feedback genuinely wants to receive it. But it's important to learn the mindset of leaders skilled at gathering feedback. They have common defining features.

- THEY REGARD FEEDBACK AS OPPORTUNITY
  (How do others view my performance?)
- THEY ARE OPEN AND NONDEFENSIVE
  (I asked the question, and want to listen to the answer.)
- THEY ARE INTERESTED IN ALTERNATIVES
  (What specifically can I do differently going forward?)

> "WE NEED VERY STRONG EARS TO HEAR OURSELVES JUDGED FRANKLY, AND BECAUSE THERE ARE FEW WHO CAN ENDURE FRANK CRITICISM WITHOUT BEING STUNG BY IT, THOSE WHO VENTURE TO CRITICIZE US PERFORM A REMARKABLE ACT OF FRIENDSHIP, FOR TO UNDERTAKE TO WOUND OR OFFEND A MAN FOR HIS OWN GOOD IS TO HAVE A HEALTHY LOVE FOR HIM."
>
> — MICHEL DE MONTAIGNE

Just as you may be apprehensive about getting feedback, others often experience as much (or more) uneasiness about giving it, an issue we will tackle in the next chapter. Someone needs to make the first move, and in many cases that person is the feedback receiver. (For more on the mindset that drives feedback-seeking, see Chapters 4 and 5.)

Here, we'd like to focus on the mindset that informs what happens after the feedback is delivered.

If you react to and subsequently act on what you're told in the right way, you can benefit fully from its value. Just as important, your behavior sends a signal to others about how you've received the feedback. This either motivates them or discourages them to help you in the future. If you truly desire ongoing, proactive feedback from others, follow through on SBI (situation-behavior-impact). Mindset is critical to shaping how you react to and act on the feedback you're given.

EVALUATE BEFORE YOU ACT

Anytime you receive feedback from someone, even someone who has given you relevant insights in the past, take a minute or two after the interaction to evaluate the content. Only you can make a judgment as to the relevance of any information you receive. Not all feedback is useful; only you can determine to what extent you want to act on other people's perceptions. Sometimes low-impact feedback comes from sources that are usually reliable and consistent. Conversely, sometimes high-impact feedback comes from sources who have been inconsistent, even unreliable. Use the following self-management model for evaluation.

ACCURACY. Who is giving you this feedback? What are their intentions, and how much do you respect this person's opinion?

VALUE. Do you like this feedback or not? Is this something that can be helpful to you? Do you want to know more?

IMPORTANCE. What are you going to do about it? Anything? Not all feedback can or should be acted upon. On the other hand, some feedback cannot be ignored.

If you are unsure about the accuracy and value of the feedback, check with a trusted colleague.

DON'T: Become defensive or explain your behavior. (You can either spend your time mobilizing your defenses or you can spend your time listening. Defending your actions is counterproductive, whereas listening is extremely useful.)

DO: Ask the person to give you alternatives to your behavior.

PUT THE FEEDBACK IN ITS PROPER PLACE
(But Don't Store It There Permanently)

Once you've evaluated the accuracy, value, and importance of the feedback, file it accordingly. Should you fully embrace and act on it immediately? Or perhaps mull it over and seek more perspective before making changes? Or is it something that, for now, you will choose not to act on?

Notice that we said "for now" and didn't say "reject" or "discard." Remember, experience is dynamic and future events (or even the subsequent memory of past events) might cause you to look at that feedback differently. So don't file it away permanently; leave it open to future consideration.

Finally, be prepared for additional feedback from that person. Depending on what you do with it, they may be compelled to give more, either to reinforce progress or remind you of the impact of your behavior.

THE TOOLSET for
GATHERING
ONGOING FEEDBACK:
Feedback Checklist

Here are some pointers you can use to remind yourself of the important steps whenever you seek feedback from others.

- ☐ Seek feedback on a regular basis. Exchanging information and perceptions is a process, not a single event.

- ☐ Seek feedback after you have identified your goals. Access others in short, concise sessions.

- ☐ Always seek specific feedback. Use the SBI model to accomplish this.

- ☐ Don't make excuses or try to explain your behavior. When receiving feedback, remain calm and be sure to say, "Thank you."

- [ ] When receiving feedback, be sure to ask for alternative behaviors to improve your performance.

- [ ] Be prepared to paraphrase and summarize any feedback you receive.

- [ ] Be sure to respect individuals who don't wish to give feedback. They may change their minds later, so leave the door open.

- [ ] Be sure to take the time after the feedback interaction to evaluate the information.

- [ ] One of the more important uses of feedback is to teach yourself to recognize situations in which you need to alter a certain behavior. Feedback can be used to "catch yourself" at times when you are not performing at your best.

- [ ] Use feedback to clarify goals, to track progress toward those goals, and to improve the effectiveness of your behaviors over a period of time.

KEY TAKEAWAYS in
GATHERING
ONGOING FEEDBACK

- ASK FOR FEEDBACK FROM THE RIGHT PEOPLE.

- ASK AT THE RIGHT TIME.

- ASK IN THE RIGHT WAY.

- ASK OFTEN.

- EVALUATE BEFORE YOU ACT ON THE FEEDBACK.

- PUT FEEDBACK IN ITS PROPER PLACE.

- STAY OPEN TO REEXAMINING FEEDBACK.

CHAPTER ELEVEN

DELIVERING ONGOING FEEDBACK

After one of the great vaudeville comedians of the early twentieth century transitioned to movies, he used a running gag to open an early film. In the scene a stagehand rushes into Lou Holtz's backstage dressing room to exclaim, "You're on!"

The comedian looks up and asks, "Oh. How am I doing?"

That is the age-old question, and no matter what level you occupy in an organization, from line manager to senior executive to team leader—even stagehand—it's a question you'll need to answer. The skill of giving meaningful and effective feedback, the focus of this chapter, is important because it helps people develop and, ultimately, it gets the work done.

Whereas the previous chapter examined how to solicit feedback, we are turning the tables here to examine how we give feedback. Having established the supreme importance of communication in the workplace, and the make-or-break role of feedback, we now know some of the values of quality, usable feedback:

- FEEDBACK IS BASED ON OBSERVATION.
- ITS MESSAGE IS SPECIFIC AND DIRECT.
- IT ENABLES THE RECEIVER TO UNDERSTAND THE PRECISE IMPACT OF HER OR HIS BEHAVIOR.
- IT CAN MOTIVATE THE RECEIVER TO START, STOP, OR CONTINUE BEHAVIOR THAT AFFECTS PERFORMANCE.

This chapter explains how to deliver effective feedback by showing how to build your message, when to deliver it, and how to communicate it. By using the methods and examples we offer, your feedback can become a tool for development—for others and yourself.

MEASURING BEHAVIOR

As a manager, you no doubt spend a good deal of time on numbers, wrestling with an unwieldy amount of information about factors that affect your business: What is my division's revenue versus expenses for the quarter and what is driving expenses up? What percentage of our quota has my division achieved year to date and what is left in the pipeline? What is our current production level and how can we increase capacity in the short term?

Managers deal in numbers because they are specific and quantifiable and can be used as goals. Yet oftentimes the same managers who develop specific "What if" scenarios in response to numbers, and examine business data like scientists with microscopes, use no such specifics when evaluating the company's most important capital: employee performance.

The question is, How can we apply the same analytical rigor and attention that we use to understand business information to give feedback?

Think of feedback you may have heard (or given) in the past.

- "HE IS A GOOD LEADER."

- "SHE COMMUNICATES WELL."

- "HE NEEDS TO BE MORE STRATEGIC."

The intent of such statements is to be helpful. But how helpful can statements be that evaluate or interpret but don't go on to describe the "because"—the specific behavior observed—so that the recipient of the feedback might learn and develop by repeating or avoiding that behavior? All three examples above beg the question of what caused the speaker to create the feedback message.

- WHAT DID YOUR BOSS DO THAT MADE YOU THINK HE WAS A GOOD LEADER?

- WHAT DID YOUR TEAM LEADER SAY (AND HOW DID SHE SAY IT) TO MAKE YOU THINK SHE COMMUNICATES WELL?

- WHAT DID YOUR SUBORDINATE DO THAT MADE YOU CONCLUDE HIS THINKING WASN'T STRATEGIC ENOUGH?

"EFFECTIVE FEEDBACK IS NOT PRAISE OR CRITICISM.
IT IS CAREFULLY CHOSEN LANGUAGE AND ACTIONS
THAT PROPEL THE LEARNER FORWARD."
- REGIE ROUTMAN

FOLLOWING A PROCESS

Feedback all comes down to a conversation—but potentially a conversation that is a memorable and far-reaching experience in our working lives. The right feedback at the right time, delivered in the right way, can change the course of a project, a career, maybe even a business.

Let's face it, giving others feedback—positive or negative— is challenging in itself and takes courage and honesty. But knowing how much is riding on feedback, you want to make the most of the opportunity.

That is where learning and following a process helps guide us, and the more skilled we become in following the process, the more comfortable it becomes. For decades at CCL, we have taught a research-based, practice-tested process for delivering feedback that has stood the test of time. We break it down to three essential steps and provide multiple tips and tools.

Before learning more about the mindset, skillset, and toolset that support delivering ongoing feedback, consider the ten behaviors listed below that typify a leader skilled at delivering feedback; identify the three that you feel you are currently strongest in and the corresponding three that you feel are most in need of development.

STRENGTH	NEED	
☐	☐	Recognizes the importance of giving feedback to others.
☐	☐	Gives appropriate feedback to others.
☐	☐	Gives feedback to others at the appropriate moment.
☐	☐	Gives feedback to others in the appropriate manner.
☐	☐	Gives feedback related to specific situations.
☐	☐	Gives feedback that describes specific behaviors.
☐	☐	Gives feedback that describes the impact of the behavior.
☐	☐	Delivers only firsthand feedback.
☐	☐	Verifies that feedback is clearly received by others.
☐	☐	Follows up with additional feedback as needed.

Take a moment to reflect on how your perceived strengths and corresponding development needs in this area have played out in the past and currently. As you progress through this chapter, keep in mind how you might augment or leverage these approaches.

BRINGING FEEDBACK OUT OF THE CLOUDS AT ADOBE

The company that boasts of "changing the world" through software such as Photoshop and Creative Cloud set about changing itself in 2012 with a decidedly low-tech tool: tough, regular discussions between managers and struggling employees.

Calculating that annual reviews devoured 80,000 hours of managers' time each year but resulted mainly in lower morale and higher employee turnover, Adobe dispensed with performance evaluations in favor of frequent one-on-one "check-ins." In these meetings, managers communicate expectations, deliver and gather feedback, and counsel employee development. Rolling surveys meanwhile measure how well managers follow their feedback training.

Within two years of the change, the company saw dramatic results in reanimating its workforce, increasing accountability, and meeting issues of frustration and dysfunction head-on. This was no small task. As an Adobe HR executive told Stanford researcher Bob Sutton, involuntary departures rose by 50 percent because regular check-ins forced managers to have frequent conversations about performance with struggling employees, rather than putting them off for annual performance reviews. At the same time, attrition dropped by 30 percent, and a strong majority of employees (78 percent) now reported that their managers were available to give feedback and discuss problems. For those employees who still chose to leave Adobe, the company told Sutton, a higher proportion was considered, in the polite parlance of HR, "nonregrettable."

How might devoting more effort to delivering ongoing feedback lead to different results for you, your team, and the organization?

> "THEY MAY FORGET YOUR NAME,
> BUT THEY WILL NEVER FORGET HOW YOU MADE THEM FEEL".
> - MAYA ANGELOU

THE MINDSET of
DELIVERING
ONGOING FEEDBACK

During many CCL programs we ask managers and executives this question:

"HOW MANY OF YOU GIVE GOOD, CONSISTENT FEEDBACK TO THE PEOPLE YOU WORK WITH?"

Usually, only one or two people raise their hands. Why so few? The explanations vary, but we often hear: "It's hard to do," or "I am afraid I will say something I will regret," or "People get emotional when they hear things they don't like," or "It might jeopardize my work relationships."

These concerns are valid, but they all stem from common mistakes that people make when giving feedback. Some of these mistakes result from a flawed mindset and can be easily redirected into more constructive thoughts. Outlined below are some common limiting mindsets and the alternative liberating mindsets that can channel your mental energy in the right direction.

LIMITING MINDSET:

EVALUATING THE INDIVIDUAL. Probably the most common mistake people make in giving feedback is putting it in judgmental terms. If you say to someone, "You were too abrasive" or "You need to be a better team player," you send a strong message about what you think is "right" or "wrong" and that you've judged this person as falling short of expectations. Judgmental feedback puts people on the defensive. By the time the words are out of your mouth, your feedback recipient is already thinking, "Who do you think you are calling me abrasive?" The energy spent defending themselves from your attack defeats any chance of a useful conversation.

LIBERATING MINDSET:

EVALUATING THE INDIVIDUAL'S BEHAVIOR. Focus your attention on the person's behavior and its impact on you, not what their behavior may or may not indicate about them as a person. Think in terms of verbs, not adjectives. For example, you might say, "Bertrand leaned closer to Nigel, raised his voice, and began pounding the table"—not "Bertrand got really angry at Nigel."

LIMITING MINDSET:

CHANNELING OTHERS' PERCEPTIONS. To say, "Sheila said that you seem confused about your new assignment" or "People are telling me that they feel like you are micromanaging them" isn't effective feedback. At best the recipient will be perplexed by such statements and wonder where coworkers got such a notion or who is talking behind closed doors. At worst he or she may be embarrassed that such a comment came through you, a third party, and resent coworkers for making it in the first place. The person receiving the feedback is likely to become defensive and unable to hear your feedback.

LIBERATING MINDSET:

CHANNELING YOUR PERCEPTIONS. Deliver *your* feedback, not someone else's. Feedback needs to be authentic and accurate to have impact, so it needs to come directly from you. When others approach you with feedback about someone else, first ask them if they've shared that feedback with the other person. If not, encourage them to do so.

LIMITING MINDSET:

FOCUSING ON PERCEIVED MOTIVES. Telling someone that you know they are behaving a certain way because of an impending divorce, jealousy over a coworker's advancement, or suffering burnout is ineffective because what you think you know about someone's intents and motives is probably wrong. Feedback that goes to motive is likely to cause resentment by the recipient.

LIBERATING MINDSET:

FOCUSING ON ACTUAL IMPACT. Leave motive out of the equation. Only the individual you are giving the feedback to can truly understand why he or she did something, and if this is a behavior that is a blind spot, the person might not even be aware of his or her motives. Don't get caught up in the "Why?" of someone's behavior. Instead, focus on what their specific behavior was and the impact it had on you.

"WHATEVER WORDS WE UTTER SHOULD BE CHOSEN WITH CARE
FOR PEOPLE WILL HEAR THEM AND BE INFLUENCED BY THEM
FOR GOOD OR ILL."
- BUDDHA

THE SKILLSET of
DELIVERING ONGOING FEEDBACK:
The SBI Feedback Technique

You can avoid common feedback mistakes by learning how to communicate important information about performance to subordinates, peers, or superiors in a way that helps them listen to what you are saying and identify ways in which they can improve.

As previously discussed, during the course of giving feedback to tens of thousands of people over many years, CCL has developed a feedback technique we call SBI, shorthand for situation-behavior-impact. Using this technique, which CCL teaches to thousands of managers every year, you can deliver feedback that replaces personal attack, incorrect judgments, vague statements, and third-party slights with direct and objective comments on a person's actions.

Hearing SBI-type feedback, the recipient can more easily see what actions he or she can take to continue and improve performance or to change behavior that is ineffective or even an obstacle to performance.

The SBI technique is effective because it's simple. When giving feedback, you describe the situation, you describe the behavior you observed, and you explain the impact that the behavior had on you: simple, direct, and effective—if you learn the three steps and practice them regularly. In the following pages, we will show you how to use each component of the SBI approach.

CAPTURE THE SITUATION (S).

The first step in giving effective feedback is to capture and clarify the specific situation in which the behavior occurred. If you say, "On Tuesday, in the break room with Carol and Fred" rather than "A couple days ago at the office with some people," you avoid the vague comments and exaggerations that torpedo so many feedback opportunities. Describing the location and time of a behavior creates context for your feedback recipients, helping them remember clearly their thinking and behavior at the time. Remember, capturing the situation is only the start of your feedback session.

Here are a few examples of how you might successfully describe a situation when giving feedback:

- "YESTERDAY MORNING, WHILE WE WERE INSPECTING THE PLANT . . ."
- "LAST MONDAY, AFTER LUNCH, WHILE WE WERE WALKING WITH CINDY TO THE MEETING . . ."
- "TODAY, FIRST THING THIS MORNING, WHEN YOU AND I WERE TALKING AT THE COFFEE MACHINE . . ."
- "THIS PAST FRIDAY NIGHT, AT THE COCKTAIL PARTY FOR THE NEW MARKETING MANAGER, WHEN KARL WAS EXPLAINING HIS NEW JOB DESCRIPTION . . ."

Specificity is important when recalling a situation. The more specifics and details you can use in bringing the situation to mind, the clearer your message will be.

DON'T: Pass along vague feedback from others.

DO: Provide specific and firsthand descriptions of behavior.

DESCRIBE THE BEHAVIOR (B).

Describing behavior is the second step to giving effective feedback. It's also the most crucial step and the one most often omitted—probably because behavior can be difficult to identify and describe. The most common mistake in giving feedback happens when judgments are communicated using adjectives that describe a person but not a person's actions. That kind of feedback is ineffective because it doesn't give the receiver information about what behavior to stop or to continue in order to improve performance.

Consider the phrases below:

- HE WAS RUDE DURING THE MEETING.
- SHE WAS ENGAGED DURING THE SMALL-GROUP DISCUSSION.
- SHE SEEMED BORED AT HER TEAM'S PRESENTATION.
- HE SEEMED PLEASED WITH THE REPORT HIS EMPLOYEES PRESENTED.

These phrases describe an observer's *impression* or *interpretation* of a behavior. Now look at the following list of actions an observer might witness that would lead to those impressions and interpretations.

- HE SPOKE AT THE SAME TIME ANOTHER PERSON WAS SPEAKING. (Rude)
- SHE LEANED FORWARD IN HER CHAIR, WROTE NOTES AFTER OTHER PEOPLE SPOKE, AND THEN SAID HER THOUGHTS TO THE GROUP, REPEATING SOME OF THE THINGS THAT OTHER PEOPLE SAID. (Engaged)
- SHE YAWNED, ROLLED HER EYES, AND LOOKED OUT THE WINDOW. (Bored)
- HE SMILED AND NODDED HIS HEAD. (Pleased)

The phrases in this list use verbs to describe a person's actions. The focus is on the actual behavior, not on a judgment about what the behavior might mean. If you remember to use verbs when describing behavior, you avoid the mistake of judging behavior. By focusing on the action, not the impression, you can communicate clear facts that a person can understand and act on.

In order to become more adept at identifying behavior and, in turn, more effectively communicate what you have seen to the feedback recipient, you have to capture not only what people do but how they do it. The new CEO who stands before her company and says, "I'm excited to be your new president" will appear insincere if she has no expression on her face, speaks in a flat voice, and uses no hand gestures. So when giving people feedback using SBI, it is not only important to capture what is said or done but how it is said and done.

DON'T: Label a behavior as a problem.

DO: Acknowledge the impact of the behavior on you.

EXPLAIN THE IMPACT (I).

The final step in giving effective feedback is to relay the impact that the other person's behavior had on you. The impact you want to communicate is not how you think a person's behavior might affect the organization, coworkers, a program, clients, a product, or any other third party. The impact you want to focus on and communicate is your reaction to a behavior. There are two directions you can take when sharing the impact of a person's behavior.

- You can evaluate or make a judgment about the person's behavior: *"I thought you showed interest when you asked for the group's opinions."* This tactic is the most common, but it is also the less effective of the two because the person getting the feedback can argue with your interpretation of the behavior.

- You can acknowledge the emotional effect the person's behavior had on you. *"When you told me in the meeting that my concerns about product deadlines were 'overblown,' I felt belittled."*

The second approach can be more effective than the first because it truly is your reaction to someone's behavior, a reaction that only you experienced. The person hearing your feedback can't easily dismiss your personal experience, and so is more likely to hear what you've said.

By communicating the personal impact a behavior has had on you, you are sharing a point of view and asking the other person to view that behavior from your perspective. That kind of sharing helps to build trust, which in turn can lead to even more effective feedback as communication is improved. If you have difficulty finding the right word to describe the impact a behavior has had on you, take a look at the Impact Words tool below.

DON'T: Give advice unless asked.

DO: Give your feedback and then stop talking.

THE TOOLSET for
DELIVERING
ONGOING FEEDBACK:
Impact Words

Getting just the right word to express the impact a behavior has on you is important. The right word can help keep your feedback from being vague or misconstrued. Finding the right word, however, isn't always easy. To help you put impact into words that you can deliver as effective feedback, we compiled this list of descriptive impact words.

Ambivalent	Fearful	Intimidated	Pressured	Tempted
Angry	Flustered	Isolated	Proud	Tense
Annoyed	Foolish	Jealous	Refreshed	Tentative
Astounded	Frantic	Kind	Rejected	Terrible
Betrayed	Frightened	Left Out	Relaxed	Terrified
Bored	Frustrated	Lonely	Relieved	Threatened
Burdened	Glad	Low	Restless	Tired
Calm	Good	Mad	Rewarded	Troubled
Captivated	Gratified	Miserable	Sad	Uneasy
Challenged	Happy	Nervous	Satisfied	Unsettled
Diminished	Helpful	Odd	Scared	Vehement
Disturbed	Helpless	Outraged	Shocked	Vital
Divided	Honored	Overwhelmed	Skeptical	Vulnerable
Ecstatic	Hurt	Peaceful	Spiteful	Welcome
Electrified	Ignored	Persecuted	Startled	Wonderful
Empty	Impressed	Petrified	Stupid	Worried
Excited	Infuriated	Pleasant	Sure	
Exhausted	Inspired	Pleased	Sympathetic	

DON'T: Sandwich your negative feedback between positive messages.

DO: Focus on a single message.

KEY TAKEAWAYS in DELIVERING ONGOING FEEDBACK

- CAPTURE THE SITUATION (S).
- DESCRIBE THE BEHAVIOR (B).
- EXPLAIN THE IMPACT (I).
- CHOOSE THE APPROPRIATE WORDS.
- EVALUATE BEHAVIOR, NOT THE PERSON.
- DESCRIBE YOUR PERCEPTIONS, NOT THOSE OF OTHERS.
- FOCUS ON IMPACT, NOT MOTIVES.

CHAPTER TWELVE

MAPPING YOUR LEADERSHIP IDENTITY

In our era of globalization, the world is getting smaller. It means that people of different identities are in closer contact than ever before, and that is a leadership challenge.

Identity comprises the parts of a person's self that come from belonging to particular groups—some visible, others less apparent. They include age, ethnicity, race, religion, nationality, and socioeconomic status.

WHETHER YOU ARE AWARE OF IT OR NOT, IDENTITY INFORMS HOW YOU LEAD.

Likewise, the identities of those around you affect how they view you as a leader and how they view and work with others. This chapter will help you develop your awareness of identity, the role it plays in your workplace, and how it can be leveraged to create positive outcomes.

So how can we begin to think of our and others' identities? Identity, which is diverse and often nuanced, can be usefully defined using the following three categories:

GIVEN IDENTITY

The attributes or conditions that you have no choice about are your given identity. They may be characteristics you were born with, or they may have been given to you in childhood or later in life. Elements of your given identity include birthplace, age, ethnicity, birth order, physical characteristics and abilities, certain family roles, and possibly religion.

CHOSEN IDENTITY

These are the characteristics that you choose. They may describe your status as well as attributes and skills. Your occupation, hobbies, political affiliation, place of residence, family roles, and religion may all be chosen.

CORE IDENTITY

These are the attributes that you think make you unique as an individual. Some will change over the course of your lifetime; others may remain constant. Elements of your core identity may include traits, behaviors, beliefs, values, and skills.

SKILL SET

OCCUPATION

AGE

HOME

Some attributes may overlap or appear in two categories. Different people might put the same aspect of their identity in different categories depending on how much of a choice it felt like to them. For instance, your religious affiliation could be seen as either a given or a chosen aspect of your identity.

Many attributes are also subjective. One person's interpretation of *educated* may not match another's definition. Some may assume that you have chosen certain characteristics when, from your vantage point, you had little or no choice. Perhaps you were expected to go into the family business and never really made a choice about your profession.

Finally, context is important. Parts of your identity that matter to you may not matter to others or may matter only in certain situations. Aspects of your identity that seem insignificant to you could become huge benefits or obstacles when you are working in certain situations or with particular groups. In your own country you may leverage local culture to build rapport with others, but when traveling to other countries, you may downplay your culture and leverage your education and career credentials.

With awareness of identity we have clearer, richer interactions with others. It helps us to:

UNDERSTAND WHO WE ARE AND WHO OTHERS ARE.

CHALLENGE ASSUMPTIONS ABOUT OURSELVES AND OTHERS.

ARTICULATE WHAT MATTERS MOST.

SEEK COMMON GROUND.

USE DIFFERENCES POSITIVELY.

CREATE SHARED DIRECTION, ALIGNMENT, AND COMMITMENT.

DECREASE THE LIKELIHOOD OF MISUNDERSTANDING.

INCREASE YOUR OPENNESS TO DIFFERENT PERSPECTIVES.

MORE ACCURATELY INTERPRET SITUATIONS THAT CALL ON YOUR ABILITY TO LEAD.

Consider the ten behaviors listed below that typify a leader with a solid grasp of identity; identify the three that you feel you are currently strongest in and the corresponding three that you feel are most in need of development.

STRENGTH	NEED	
☐	☐	Maintains a clear sense of his or her identity.
☐	☐	Considers how others perceive his or her identity.
☐	☐	Understands how his or her identity contributes to leader effectiveness.
☐	☐	Examines his or her perceptions of others' identity.
☐	☐	Understands the role identity can play in interactions.
☐	☐	Values those with identities that differ from his or hers.
☐	☐	Spots potential identity conflicts quickly.
☐	☐	Directly addresses conflicts that arise from different identities.
☐	☐	Promotes interaction among people with different identities.
☐	☐	Creates an inclusive environment where different identities are accepted.

Take a moment to reflect on how your perceived strengths and corresponding development needs in this area have played out in the past and currently. As you progress through this chapter, keep in mind how you might augment or leverage these approaches.

VOICES OF EXPERIENCE

POPE FRANCIS: THE UNCOMMONLY COMMON MAN

As of 2016, he didn't own a cell phone. Nor did he know how to use a computer. So how did Argentine-born Pope Francis become the most popular leader in the world, transcending ideology, politics, region, socioeconomics, and, not least of all, religion?

Rather than focusing solely on the 1.2 billion members of his own group, the head of the world's largest organization instead turned his attention to engaging those outside his group: people of other faiths and people without organized religion.

The signature of his papacy, small and seemingly unscripted gestures that belie his position, began when he greeted the crowd awaiting his first appearance after being named pope with two simple words: "Buona sera," good morning. Living in guest quarters at the Vatican, traveling and speaking frequently, Francis has engaged others rather than insulated himself.

The pope's interactions with common people—including the homeless, sick, and disabled—increased his appeal and credibility as a leader who looks past boundaries to see people's commonalities rather than differences.

How might the pope's example of humbleness and inclusivity give you insight into how you can engage others as a leader to remove the barriers sometimes created by differing identities?

THE MINDSET for
MAPPING YOUR LEADERSHIP IDENTITY

The social identity theory developed by Henri Tajfel and John Turner says we use identity to:

CATEGORIZE people into groups based on a shared belief, experience, or characteristic (for example, women, engineers, Canadians).

IDENTIFY with certain groups ourselves.

COMPARE the groups we belong to with other groups, typically thinking more highly of our own groups.

How we *categorize* people is a complex, subjective process. For instance, you may believe that religion is one of the most important aspects of a person's identity, so you group people by, and possibly make assumptions about, their religious affiliation. Someone else might not care about or even think about another person's religious affiliation and would therefore give more weight to another social identity—for example, nationality.

The groups you *identify* with are the ones that you tend to feel most at home with. The behaviors and attributes typical of these groups are what feel normal (read *preferable*) to you. The coupling between self and identity groups is often powerful, resulting in a bright line being drawn between those who belong with you and those who do not.

We are more likely to assess people in our own groups by their intentions, which suggests positive attributes. On the other hand, we tend to assess people in other groups by how their behavior impacts us, suggesting negative attributes. This comparison process, often not deliberate or even conscious, is a two-way street. That means people belonging to other social identity groups are also making comparisons that may be very different from our own.

To address these potential challenges you must first develop awareness of your own identity.

Worlds Apart or Two of a Kind?

THE STORY OF AKRIT AND LAUREN

Akrit and Lauren hold similar management positions in the same organization located in the United States. Akrit was born in India to a wealthy family and has an advanced degree. Lauren was born in the U.S. to a low-income family. She entered the workforce early and has a lot of work experience but lacks the formal training that Akrit has. Lauren feels that, because Akrit is a man and has a higher education level, he is afforded more opportunities. Akrit feels that, because Lauren is a U.S. native and has been with the organization longer, she has an advantage. Each resents the other for "having it easy."

Lauren and Akrit are relating to and reacting to each other, in large part, based on their identities. The trouble is, they are only seeing one aspect of each other's overall identities. In other words, they may have more things in common than they realize.

Think about conflicts that you encounter with your colleagues at work. What about them could be attributable to different identities? How might you need to adapt your perceptions of others to better take their identities into account?

"WE SHOULDN'T JUDGE PEOPLE THROUGH THE PRISM
OF OUR OWN STEREOTYPES."
- QUEEN RANIA OF JORDAN

THE TOOLSET for
LEADERSHIP IDENTITY:
Your Identity Map

Creating a map of your identity is a way to capture and articulate how you see yourself. You can look clearly at your obvious, surface-level identity and then begin to dig deeper. This can be very useful in exploring how others perceive you as a leader—who will feel more at home with you, who will give your words more weight, and so on. Your identity map should include the three components discussed earlier:

GIVEN IDENTITY, CHOSEN IDENTITY, AND CORE IDENTITY

Instructions

1. Draw three concentric circles to represent the different categories of your identity.

2. In the outer ring, write words that describe your given identity: the attributes or conditions that you had no choice about, from birth or later. You may want to include your nationality, age, gender, physical characteristics, certain family roles, and possibly religion. Examples include female, only child, 48, tall, blind, African American, cancer patient, widower..

3. In the next ring, list aspects of your chosen identity. Consider including your occupation, hobbies, political affiliation, where you live, certain family roles, and possibly religion. Examples are cyclist, mother, engineer, expatriate, college graduate, husband, leader, Parisian, Buddhist.

4. In the center circle, write your core attributes—traits, behaviors, beliefs, values, and skills that you think make you unique as an individual. Select things that are relatively enduring about you or that are key to who you are today. For example, you may see yourself as funny, artistic, kind, conservative, attentive, creative, impatient, musical, family-focused, assertive.

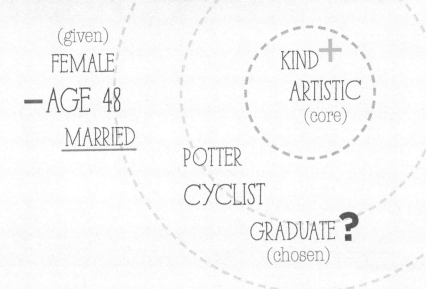

(given)
FEMALE
—AGE 48
MARRIED

KIND +
ARTISTIC
(core)

POTTER

CYCLIST

GRADUATE ?
(chosen)

AFTER YOU COMPLETE YOUR MAP:

<u>Underline the items</u> that are important to you personally. These are likely to be the terms you would use to describe yourself.

+ **Put a plus sign** beside the items that you believe contribute to your ability to lead effectively in your organization.

— **Put a minus sign** beside the items that you believe detract from your ability to lead effectively in your organization.

? **Put a question mark** beside the items that may vary in how they affect your leadership ability, depending on context.

INTERPRETING YOUR MAP

Refer to your map while answering the following questions to examine your identity in more depth.

- When you look at the underlined items on your map, what trends do you see? Are they mainly part of your given, chosen, or core identity?

- When you look at the items with pluses, minuses, and question marks, what trends do you see? Are they mainly part of your given, chosen, or core identity?

- Of the aspects with pluses, minuses, and question marks, which are things you have in common with other people in the organization? Which are things that only you or a very small number of people possess? What are the leadership implications?

- What aspects of your identity help you make connections with people at work? What aspects of your identity get in the way of making connections with people at work? What gives you the impression that this is the case?

- Are there aspects of your identity that you keep hidden at work? What impact might that have on you and those around you?

- How might you reveal or emphasize particular elements of your identity at work in order to build or improve relationships?

- How might you hide or deemphasize particular elements of your identity at work in order to build or improve relationships?

THE SKILLSET for
MAPPING YOUR
LEADERSHIP IDENTITY

SEEK ANOTHER PERSPECTIVE

Share your identity map with someone you trust and whose opinion you value. Your partner may or may not see your map the same way you do, but that's the whole point. There is no right or wrong interpretation.

Follow these instructions:

1. **Show your partner** your completed identity map.

2. **Discuss with your partner:**

   - aspects of your identity that you believe help you make connections with people at work
   - aspects of your identity that you believe impede making connections at work

3. **Then, ask your partner:**

   - Are you surprised to see anything on my map?
   - Are there aspects I have left off the map that impact how others perceive me?

"KNOW WHO YOU ARE, WHO YOU WANT TO BE,
AND START TALKING AND WORKING WITH WHOM YOU ARE NOT."
- TARIQ RAMADAN

CREATE ROUTINE CONTACT

The simplest and perhaps best known strategy for leveraging identities involves constructing situations so that individual members of different groups come into contact with and get to know one another. Arrange opportunities for personal interaction among supervisors and subordinates and among team members, such as social events, retreats, or team-building activities. This creates more opportunity for one-to-one interactions that are based on individual people rather than the categories they fall into.

MIX IT UP

Either randomly or systematically rotate work group roles in a way that involves people from different identity groups. Again, this softens boundaries between groups, and individuals have more opportunities for interpersonal interaction.

IDENTIFY WITH THE ORGANIZATION

Foster a collective identity by emphasizing that everyone belongs to the same organization and is working toward a common goal. The organization becomes an all-inclusive identity group, and differences between groups are minimized.

SHARE THE STATUS

If groups are tightly formed around identity, create situations in which different groups are given equal status. Structure a project or a team so that members of each group have distinct but complementary roles in reaching common goals. This strategy is potentially risky, because differences between groups are made apparent. But if the situation is handled well, individuals learn that they can maintain their group identity and also value another group's unique contributions.

CREATE AN INCLUSIVE ENVIRONMENT

Organizational elements such as policies, practices, and the organizational climate support inclusiveness. Inclusiveness policies and practices that encourage an open dialogue about problems stemming from identity conflict may be helpful. Policies of zero tolerance for fighting, harassment, and discrimination do work. Also, mechanisms for allowing identity issues to emerge in safe and orchestrated ways may be effective. Of course, it is critical to consider the country's culture and laws when determining a suitable remedy for addressing identity conflicts.

TAKE ACTION

Problems started by identity conflicts can become worse when they are ignored. Early actions help to minimize disruptive outcomes. What specific action to take depends very much on the country and cultural situation, but allowing a situation to continue without intervention invites greater trouble.

KEY TAKEAWAYS in

MAPPING YOUR
LEADERSHIP IDENTITY

STAY AWARE OF THE INFLUENCE OF CATEGORIZING, IDENTIFYING, AND COMPARING.

CREATE ROUTINE CONTACT BETWEEN DIFFERENT GROUPS.

ROTATE WORK GROUP ROLES.

FOSTER A COLLECTIVE ORGANIZATIONAL IDENTITY.

SHARE STATUS AMONG DIFFERENT GROUPS.

CREATE AN INCLUSIVE ENVIRONMENT.

TAKE ACTION WHEN IDENTITY CONFLICTS OCCUR.

CHAPTER THIRTEEN

DEMONSTRATING POLITICAL SAVVY

Politics in the workplace is an undeniable fact of life. How you engage in politics is under your control. You can do this effectively, given the right skills.

People describe politics in their organization as everything from coalition-building to back-stabbing. But the truth is, organizational politics is neither good nor bad; it's simply the air we breathe in organizations.

Your perception of organizational politics shapes how you respond to it. It can also influence how you feel about the organization and your coworkers and how well you do your job. One way to be effective in the inherently political environment of contemporary organizations is to change your way of understanding politics—to become politically savvy. To develop and demonstrate "political intelligence."

Politics, because it is complex and changing, requires savvy. You can either try to avoid politics (which is impossible) or engage in it reluctantly and accept that politics will exert its influence on you. Or you can embrace politics and commit to building your political skills so that you can leverage politics to your advantage and in service of your team, the organization, and other stakeholders.

Here's a breakdown of behaviors that typify a politically savvy leader. Of the ten behaviors listed below, identify the three that you feel you are currently strongest in and the corresponding three that you feel are most in need of development.

STRENGTH	NEED	
☐	☐	Understands the political nature of the organization.
☐	☐	Accepts politics as a natural part of organizational life.
☐	☐	Engages in organizational politics.
☐	☐	Sees politics as neither good nor bad.
☐	☐	Builds relationships through networking.
☐	☐	Controls impulses.
☐	☐	Reads situations accurately.
☐	☐	Responds constructively to disagreements.
☐	☐	Comes across as authentic.
☐	☐	Inspires others to have trust and confidence in him or her.

Take a moment to reflect on how your perceived strengths and corresponding development needs in this area have played out in the past and currently. As you progress through this chapter, keep in mind how you might augment or leverage these approaches.

THE USES OF POLITICAL SAVVY:
A PRIME MINISTER ON YOUR SIDE

He had been Norway's prime minister since World War II, having served longer than anyone in that position, and he was the only world leader known to have stepped down due to the illness of depression. But the lines on Kjell Magne Bondevik's leadership resume continued to grow after he left politics in 2005. In many respects, his increasing effectiveness as a leader stems from his mastery of the political system.

Bondevik's openness about his depression changed the way Norwegians talk about mental illness. As he told the Bulletin of the World Health Organization: "They were thinking: 'If the prime minister can talk about his mental health problems, why can't we do it too?'" Awareness then turned to action. Bondevik, a longtime leader of the Christian Democratic Party, used his knowledge of the health-care system and its stakeholders to effectively advocate for funding a massive overhaul of the neglected system.

The former prime minister's efforts were not limited to domestic policy. He became a UN humanitarian envoy to the Horn of Africa and meanwhile founded the Oslo Center for Peace and Human Rights. The center provided democratic assistance in Kenya, Somalia, the Sudan, and Burma.

Bondevik's journey illustrates how political leadership skills can help people cross boundaries and forge creative alliances. How can you develop political savvy that will make you a more effective leader?

THE MINDSET of the
POLITICALLY
SAVVY LEADER

Mindset often stands in the way of developing political savvy. Common beliefs such as the following contribute to a negative perception of politics and encourage avoidance:

- POLITICS IS BAD.
- POLITICS IS A WIN-LOSE GAME.
- POLITICS IS ABOUT BEING FALSE.

Politically savvy leaders see things differently. They adopt a practical and realistic perspective that encourages them to use their political skills, behaviors, and qualities to be effective and accomplish shared objectives. They value sincerity as a vital element in their approach and work hard to build confidence and trust. Following are some of the key mindsets of politically savvy leaders.

POLITICS IS NEUTRAL AND NATURAL

Engaging in politics can lead to desired outcomes while also being positive and authentic. Many politically savvy leaders have developed high-quality relationships and networks, know themselves well, and have a good sense about what is going on around them. They get the resources that they and their subordinates or teams need to function effectively.

They also clearly see politics around them, where employees experience competing interests, scarce resources, ambiguity in decision making and authority, unclear rules and regulations to govern workplace behavior, and a lack of information. But politics to them is not a zero-sum game where they work the system to their own advantage and to the disadvantage of others. They regard workplace politics as neutral. They understand workplace realities and use that knowledge to influence others to act in ways that enhance personal and organizational objectives.

Once you consider, understand, and accept that organizational politics is neutral and a natural part of everyday occurrences in the workplace, you can appropriately build your capacity to lead effectively in that environment. You can be regarded as someone with effective political savvy in your organization, one who can influence and persuade others in a sincere, authentic manner.

NETWORKING WORKS

Leaders who possess a strong networking ability build cooperative, beneficial relationships with their colleagues. Networking comes easily to some people, while for others it feels like a political move. If you are among the latter, consider changing your thinking. In other words, think of networking as a way to build and enhance a support group of diverse people. If that doesn't sell the idea, think of the social capital you build by networking as a critical factor to your success and that of your team.

Your network probably includes peers and other people over whom you have no direct authority. To lead in contemporary organizations, you need to develop the ability to influence others in order to accomplish your organization's work. Although this may not be new to you, the recognition that you already know how to negotiate and manage conflict among your peer networks is a step toward building your political savvy. (For more on developing your networking skills, see Chapter 18.)

"THERE IS A DIFFERENCE BETWEEN COZYING UP TO POWER
AND BEING CLOSE TO POWER."
- BONO

THINK FIRST

Count to ten, think twice before speaking, choose your battles—how many times have you heard or said one of these? Chances are there have been a lot. Impulse control is important, and it can also help you avoid a mistake like sharing an idea prematurely, shooting down another person's idea, telling an inappropriate joke, or using humor at the wrong time.

Direct reports characterize managers who lack impulse control as hostile, aggressive, and intolerant—especially when things don't go the manager's way. Do you tend to remain calm in a crisis and when recovering from mistakes, or do you let your anger escalate and lead you down a path where you lose composure?

THE SKILLSET of the
POLITICALLY SAVVY LEADER

In some organizations it may be difficult to discuss workplace politics, much less to ask for help in developing political savvy. Even if you work in such an organization, there's still hope. In this section we provide simple ideas and exercises to help you accentuate skills, behaviors, and qualities that are vital to being effective in political environments.

MINGLE STRATEGICALLY

The ability to build strategic relationships and garner support is important for the success of any leader. When it comes to building political savvy, it is essential. The easiest way to get started is to look at your current network. When you hear the word *networking*, you may think of handing out business cards, going to a networking or professional event, or even schmoozing. Networking goes far beyond that. Try the following techniques:

- Be proactive in telling your boss what is going on, where struggles are and where things are going well. With this information, your boss won't be blindsided, and trust, rapport, and relationships can build.

- Identify people in your organization who are already politically savvy. Notice whom they network with and how they behave and carry themselves. Such observation and modeling can be very helpful in building your own savvy.

- Look for a mentor or coach to help you build your network. Think of this opportunity in terms of your current leadership role and your longer-term career goals. Being politically savvy can benefit both.

CAUTION! If you manage others, don't spend so much time building your network upward and outward that you forget to develop and manage your direct reports.

'LEADERSHIP IS THE ART OF GETTING SOMEONE ELSE TO DO SOMETHING YOU WANT DONE BECAUSE HE WANTS TO DO IT.'
- DWIGHT EISENHOWER

READ THE SITUATION

Politically savvy managers tend to be perceptive observers of others and of social situations. This kind of social astuteness involves observation, self-awareness, and the ability to adapt and tailor behavior to different environmental conditions. Here are some ways to more effectively read what's going on around you.

- Pay attention to the nonverbal behaviors of those around you. Many times, it's not the actual words that matter but the feelings behind those words. People can pay more attention to nonverbal behaviors (such as gestures, postures, tone of voice, eye contact, and facial expressions) than words, particularly if the words are in direct contrast to the actions. Paying attention to the nonverbal cues in the room can help you read the situation and understand how people are really feeling.

- Practice active listening (see Chapter 9). You must be able to listen to others in order to understand them.

- Think about how others might be feeling at the moment, what is happening to them, and what circumstances are bringing them to you.

- Pay attention to your feelings and reactions. In other words, be in the moment. If in doubt, ask trusted colleagues who shared the same experience what they thought and experienced. Look beyond your own ideas, needs, and agendas and consider other people's situations, priorities, and needs.

- Consider what you can give people, understand how and why your request may have a negative effect on others, and find a way to appeal to the common good.

CAUTION! Reading the situation can take time, but over-examination can lead to action avoidance if you're not careful.

BE CONSTRUCTIVE, NOT DESTRUCTIVE

When figuring out how to handle disagreements or influence others, take a step back, gain perspective, and write down what you think would happen if you behave a certain way. Think about what others would think of you if you went with one action versus another. Also, write down what you think others are thinking or feeling in the situation. In other words, what are their perspectives? Understanding their perspectives can help you figure out what you should do in the situation. You may even want to go so far as to ask others what they are thinking or feeling to help you gain more perspective. Also consider these approaches to manage difficult situations:

- Consider working with a coach who can help you identify your hot buttons—issues that cause you to feel strong emotions—and ways to more effectively respond to them.

- If, after an honest assessment, you recognize that you tend to have trouble handling your emotions in difficult situations, consider attending an anger-management or conflict-management workshop. Such a workshop can help you set boundaries and control triggers that lead to outbursts and get you into trouble. Look for workshops that include assessment, feedback, modeling of new skills, practice of new skills, and ongoing support (so you won't lapse back into your old ways).

- Take a personality assessment. The knowledge you gain may help you understand how your personality preferences influence your behavior in response to various situations and people. You can identify skills and behaviors that contribute to your political savvy and see what you are doing that prevents or undermines your effectiveness at work.

CAUTION! Be careful that you don't overcorrect
and avoid or smooth over conflict
for the sake of harmony or personal gain.

"BUILD YOUR OPPONENT A GOLDEN BRIDGE TO RETREAT ACROSS."
- SUN TZU

LEAVE THEM WITH A GOOD IMPRESSION

What kind of impression do you make on others? Do they consider you trustworthy? Whether or not you consider yourself politically savvy, you may have thought of workplace politics as manipulation.

When asked if you want to manipulate your colleagues to get the much-needed funds for a top-priority project, you're likely to say no. But when asked if you could influence them in some way to get the funds, you probably would say yes.

Manipulation is one form of influence that can alienate your colleagues even if it is considered a justifiable means to an end. Politically astute managers struggle in these situations, but they have learned that being authentic—honest, sincere, trustworthy, and genuine—inspires others to trust and have confidence in them. Enhance your authenticity with these approaches:

- Ask friends, coworkers, advisors, mentors, or coaches you trust to give you honest feedback on their perception of your style of influence. Are you able to exert influence in a manner that does not appear or feel manipulative, insincere, or backhanded?

- Pay attention to your nonverbal behaviors (eye contact, facial expressions, body language). Keep eye contact; don't look at your watch or stare out the window when you are supposed to be listening. Make sure that your actions and words are in alignment.

- Follow through on your promises. Sometimes this can be as simple as paying attention so that you do not overcommit.

- Make appeals based on logic, emotion, or a sense of cooperation as the situation dictates. Be agile in using all three; don't always depend on the same one.

CAUTION! Don't try too hard to impress!

THE TOOLSET for
POLITICAL SAVVY:
Map Your Political Network

Use the following worksheet to map your political network. Write your name inside the oval. Then think of the people in your network, including those you would like to get to know because of their influence, power, reputation, or ability to get or provide resources. Put the names of those you have strong or close connections with closer to your oval than those you have weak or distant connections with. Look for patterns in your connections. Also look to see whether those you have close connections with are in some way connected to those you have distant connections with and consider whether you can get to know the latter through the former.

KEY TAKEAWAYS in
DEMONSTRATING POLITICAL SAVVY

- REMEMBER THAT POLITICS IS NEUTRAL AND NATURAL.

- APPROACH NETWORKING AS A WAY TO BUILD AND ENHANCE A DIVERSE SUPPORT GROUP.

- THINK FIRST AND MANAGE YOUR IMPULSES.

- MINGLE STRATEGICALLY.

- READ THE SITUATION.

- BE CONSTRUCTIVE, NOT DESTRUCTIVE.

- MAKE AN AUTHENTIC IMPRESSION.

SECTION IV
SHAPE *YOUR FUTURE*

Located in Jordan at the nexus of Africa, Asia, and Europe, Jordan's Red Sea port city of Aqaba is a lifeline for commerce to the region and has operated for more than a millennium. But in 2003, maritime traffic had become so congested that ships were waiting an average of five days to be off-loaded, and international shipping lines suspended business with the port, costing Jordan $120 million per year.

Something had to be done, but the government could not afford an estimated $500 million to update the long-neglected facility. That was when Minister of Planning Imad Fakhoury stepped forward with a bold idea: If the bottlenecked ships could not get to Aqaba, Jordan would literally bring Aqaba to the ships. Moving the container facility up the coast would free up the ancient city for tourism, without the pollution and heavy industry of the terminal. It was win-win, and surely everyone would agree.

Not entirely. Parliament opposed the plan because it would involve private interests in a public port, and the resorts and casinos envisioned for the port city might clash with Jordanian culture. Shipping agents opposed it because their own association had run the port for as long as anyone could remember. Labor unions opposed it, concerned with job security.

But Fakhoury had studied the seaport closely. He was a Harvard-trained MBA who wrote his thesis on the problem; he was also a master scuba diver who knew Aqaba's famed 8-kilometer marine coral reef and the commercial pollution that had disturbed it.

Proposing an enterprise zone that could attract foreign investment, Fakhoury and allies, including the Jordanian king, held 20 meetings to negotiate with key stakeholders and launched a public relations campaign that communicated both progress and obstacles through the media. To address the concerns of stakeholders wary of change, Jordan agreed to maintain ownership of Aqaba and contract with a private operator for a trial period. If the contractor did not meet performance benchmarks, it would soon be apparent.

The plan was a success. The contractor improved working conditions and the cargo waiting time dropped from 129 hours to zero within a six-month period, and within a year, the facility was rated one of the top three ports in the Middle East and India. Meanwhile, in the old city, Jordan attracted $20 billion in investments in resorts and established a university of hotel management and tourism where students could gain practical experience in the industry they were studying.

Beyond the narrow geography of what occurred in this story, there were broad leadership lessons to be learned. For example, even though the catalyst for the port project was a crisis, Fakhoury had thought deeply about the problem and was not proposing a hastily drawn solution. He won buy-in and assembled a team of supporters to sell the vision. He worked diligently to communicate, understand, and address the concerns of stakeholders, and he developed a model for rapid success or failure.

In this section, we dive deeper into what it takes to actively shape your future. In Chapters 14 through 16, we cover how, in order to be an effective leader, you can build a personal leadership brand that aligns with your values and how you can communicate a long-term vision to others and learn to practice authentic ways to promote yourself. Finally, recognizing that the world is in a constant state of disruption, Chapters 17 through 19 explore how to navigate change by building trust, how to cultivate and contribute to an effective network, and how to adopt a mindset of "seeking" opportunity and growth so that your leadership journey will be unending.

CHAPTER FOURTEEN

ESTABLISHING YOUR LEADERSHIP BRAND

Have you ever wished other people knew the leadership you were capable of? Have you wondered how to communicate your leadership capabilities? Those are just two questions answered by a leadership brand.

Previously we talked about assessing your reputation and being aware of your identity. In this chapter, we focus on how to communicate your individual identity as a leader so you can attain the reputation you desire. To be helpful to you, your brand must be authentic. In other words, it must align with:

- your values and what matters most to you
- the roles and work you are spending the most time doing
- how you are interacting and exchanging with others while doing that work
- how you are seen by others for the leadership contribution you are consistently making

Building and communicating your leadership brand lets people know what they can expect from you. An authentic leadership brand creates clarity for you and others about your leadership approach and the anticipated value you bring to the work you share with them.

"THE MOST EXHAUSTING THING YOU CAN BE IS INAUTHENTIC."
- ANNE MORROW LINDBERGH

This chapter outlines a plan for building and shaping your leadership brand. The goal is for you to gain an understanding and appreciation for your leadership contributions, regardless of your work setting or role.

THE ROLE OF BRANDING

Why does a leadership brand matter? Some leaders contend that it doesn't, and they mistakenly confuse leadership branding with the shadowy realm of image management, in which scandals are digitally scrubbed and made-up flattery is deployed instead.

A powerful leadership brand can enhance your ability to achieve your career goals as well as support your efforts to build and sustain the partnerships that allow you to get things done. What's more, your leadership brand can help you attract the right mentors and sponsors to advance your career and build your network. Your brand demonstrates the value you bring to your work.

MYTH: CREATING A BRAND IS ABOUT BEING FAKE.

TRUTH: IT'S THE OPPOSITE: PROJECTING YOURSELF FULLY AS A LEADER IN A WAY THAT'S CONSISTENT WITH WHO YOU ARE AND WHAT YOU DO. IT'S ABOUT COMING ACROSS TO PEOPLE IN A WAY THAT DOES YOU AND YOUR ORGANIZATION JUSTICE.

In the business world, effective brands:

- POSSESS UNIQUE DIFFERENCES—A SET OF ATTRIBUTES OR CHARACTERISTICS.
- GENERATE EXPECTATIONS FOR THOSE WHO EXPERIENCE THE BRAND.
- DELIVER EXPERIENCES THAT MATCH EXPECTATIONS. PROVIDE RESONANCE AND RELEVANCE.

Similarly, your leadership branding should:

- IDENTIFY YOUR UNIQUENESS.
- COMMUNICATE THAT UNIQUENESS TO OTHERS.
- PROVIDE A CONSISTENT EXPERIENCE THAT MEETS EXPECTATIONS.
- MAKE EXPLICIT THAT WHICH IS IMPLICIT.

Before we delve into the mindset, skillset, and toolset for establishing your leadership brand, consider the ten behaviors listed below that typify a brand-savvy leader; identify the three that you feel you are currently strongest in and the corresponding three that you feel are most in need of development.

STRENGTH	NEED	
☐	☐	Identifies his or her desired leadership brand.
☐	☐	Aligns brand aspirations with underlying values.
☐	☐	Knows the difference between leadership brand and reputation.
☐	☐	Identifies gaps between desired leadership brand and reputation.
☐	☐	Proactively builds his or her leadership brand.
☐	☐	Leverages his or her leadership brand to shape others' expectations.
☐	☐	Regularly engages in behaviors consistent with his or her leadership brand.
☐	☐	Assess progress toward achieving his or her desired brand.
☐	☐	Periodically reevaluates leadership brand aspirations.
☐	☐	Monitors social network brand.

Take a moment to reflect on how your perceived strengths and corresponding development needs in this area have played out in the past and currently. As you progress through this chapter, keep in mind how you might augment or leverage these approaches.

VOICES OF EXPERIENCE

BUILDING A BRAND AT MEXICO'S POUNCE

Aggressive. Flexible. Change agent. The words in the LinkedIn profile for Roger Viera, CEO of the Mexican high-tech manufacturing consultancy Pounce, convey an image of a person and a company that are going places with a sense of purpose.

Viera positioned the Guadalajara firm to spot and react to megatrends such as the Internet of Things, embedded software that collects data in anything from heart monitors to voting machines to firefighting equipment. In addition to his firm, Viera also positioned himself by establishing a robust social media presence, speaking at international business events such as Chicago's Tech Week and leveraging recognition such as the Ernst & Young Entrepreneur of the Year and the Gold Prize at Frankfurt's International Arch of Europe.

Even though Viera's company grew from an IT consultancy to a rapid prototyping firm with software and manufacturing divisions, the message of his personal brand has remained cohesive:

EXPERIENCE, INNOVATION, AND FORWARD MOTION.

Taking a cue from Viera, how can you craft a brand message that is consistent but also leaves space for reinvention?

THE MINDSET of the
BRAND-SAVVY LEADER

As you work to convey an effective leadership brand, keep in mind that this is not about faking anything. It's about surfacing and polishing behaviors and skills that allow your authentic self to be most effective.

However, it's also important to remember that having an authentic brand doesn't necessarily mean that it always stays the same. Times change, and so can your brand. Approaching it as something dynamic requires ongoing investment to ensure you build a brand that is relevant and fresh.

ANTICIPATE THAT YOUR BRAND ASPIRATIONS WILL SHIFT

As your definition of career success evolves, as your values undergo subtle changes and as your perceptions shift of what type of leadership is needed for the challenges you face, your brand aspirations will change accordingly. When that happens, time to re-brand.

RECOGNIZE THAT REPUTATION-BRAND GAPS ARE NOT STATIC

As your efforts to act in accordance with your brand and your values gain traction, gaps will close and you will shift your focus to addressing other aspects of your brand. Also, as you deliberately choose to re-brand, new gaps will appear and require you to channel your efforts accordingly.

REASSESS AND RECALIBRATE

Not all of your brand-building efforts will pan out. When this happens, stop to reassess your approach. Seek some advice. Look to role models for the brand you're seeking to establish and see if there are some new or different behaviors you should emphasize. Alternately, you might reconsider your brand aspiration. Maybe it doesn't really tap into your values and your authentic self.

MYTH: PEOPLE KNOW ME. WHAT IS THERE TO MANAGE?

TRUTH: PEOPLE DON'T KNOW WHAT YOU DON'T SHOW. FOR EXAMPLE, YOU MAY HAVE AGONIZED OVER A DIFFICULT DECISION, BUT IF YOUR BEHAVIOR DOESN'T REFLECT IT, OTHERS MAY SEE YOU AS RASH AND UNCARING.

THE SKILLSET for
ESTABLISHING YOUR LEADERSHIP BRAND

The constant presence of technology can both help and hurt your brand. Going viral can be a good thing or a bad thing. The recommendations in this section are framed to the unique challenges of managing your brand in the digital age.

CULTIVATE YOUR ONLINE PRESENCE

Brand-conscious leaders are aware that they have an online footprint, and keep it up to date. In Googling your name, you may find links to articles where your name is mentioned or to sites where you have made presentations. You may find links to your corporate biography. What did you like about what you found? What do you want to change?

Your social media presence depends on your profession and your preferences. Popular professional networks like LinkedIn are a good place to start because it's a popular global network and many professionals use it to stay connected to others in their field.

Here are some steps to consider:

- Identify a few people whose online brands you admire. What do you notice? How have they articulated their value and where do they appear online that enhances this value?

- Determine your story. What do you want your online brand to say about you? What expertise and points of view do you want to identify you? Clarity and consistency of message are key as you think about your story.

- What topics and issues excite you? If you do a lot of public speaking, think about how you can leverage those opportunities into digital content for blogs, newsletters, and other online outlets.

- Consider starting a personal blog or contributing to professional blogs you admire; become a regular contributor to your corporate or alumni newsletter.

- Comment and post about articles that have influenced you.

INTEGRATE PERSONAL AND PROFESSIONAL BRANDING

Many professionals choose to keep their personal and professional activities on social media separate. As an alternative, consider thinking holistically about your leadership brand, only posting assets that reflect how you want to be perceived. Every post you make, whether personal or professional, reveals something about who you are and what you value.

MYTH: WHAT YOU SEE IS WHAT YOU GET.
TRUTH: GIVEN TODAY'S GLOBAL COMMUNICATION CHANNELS, YOUR PERSONAL INTERACTIONS ARE SOMETIMES LIMITED. A 15-MINUTE INTERACTION CAN DEFINE YOU IN ANOTHER'S EYES FOR MANY YEARS.

TOOLSET #1 for
ESTABLISHING YOUR BRAND:
Values Assessment

WHAT DO YOU STAND FOR?
LET'S START BY EXAMINING YOUR VALUES.

INSTRUCTIONS: On the next page is a list of 44 values.

- Make a paper copy of this page and cut these value labels into the set of 44.

- Sort them into five categories of **always valued**; **often valued**; **sometimes valued**; **seldom valued**; and **rarely valued.**

- Stand back and take a look at how you sorted your values. Did anything surprise you? When you look back five years, were some values categorized differently? Why?

- Look at values under "always valued" and select the top five values that most resonate.

- How are you currently demonstrating behaviors and creating expectations consistent with these values?

"BE YOURSELF. EVERYONE ELSE IS ALREADY TAKEN." - OSCAR WILDE

Achievement	Competition	Knowledge
Activity	Compassion	Location
Advancement	Courage	Love
Adventure	Creativity	Loyalty
Aesthetics	Economic Security	Order
Affiliation	Enjoyment	Personal Development
Affluence	Fame	Physical Fitness
Authority	Family	Recognition
Autonomy	Friendship	Reflection
Balance	Happiness	Responsibility
Challenge	Help Others	Self-respect
Change/Variety	Humor	Spirituality
Collaboration	Influence	Status
Community	Integrity	Wisdom
Competence	Justice	

TOOLSET #2 for
ESTABLISHING YOUR BRAND:
Imagine Your Desired Brand

Taking a close look at your current leadership brand can be eye opening. It can help you analyze your current reputation and evaluate whether it is working for you or against you in your career. Self-awareness is fundamental to defining and evaluating your leadership brand. It helps you decide what you need to keep doing, start doing, and stop doing in order to establish a brand reputation that reflects what matters most to you.

CHOOSE YOUR BRAND
What would you like your brand to show? Possibilities include humorous, considerate, empowering, credible, organized, productive, calm, flexible, well informed. What behaviors and actions would lead others to see you in this way?

WATCH AND LEARN
Think about someone you've worked for or known who has an effective leadership brand. List words that describe his or her brand. Next, consider specific ways that the person behaves that enhance his or her brand. How could you adapt the person's behavior or do something similar to create an effective leadership brand? Conversely, what might you learn from someone who has an ineffective leadership brand?

PLAN AHEAD
Look at the brand of people who have the job you'd like to have in two years. What is required of people in those roles with respect to a brand? Perhaps they need to be seen as well connected, comfortable being in the spotlight, skilled at giving media interviews or speeches, or able to engage with diverse groups of people. What could you do differently to show others that you are up for the task?

GET VISUAL

Find an image of your brand! Is there a person whose brand you admire? Find a photo of him or her and post it as a reminder. Are there other pictures or images that reflect your desired brand? A rock climber to show your willingness to take on a challenge? A painting that symbolizes the feelings you hope to convey to employees? A place that speaks of the future? Whatever symbol or picture speaks to you, keep it as a reminder and for inspiration.

FINAL TOUCHES

- Assess brand-value alignment. How well does your aspirational brand match your top five values?
- Choose a tagline. Pick something short, clear, and powerful.
- Now summarize your brand as follows:

Your name: _____

Your tagline: _____

_____

The services you are uniquely suited for delivering to your customers:

_____

_____

The top five values phrased as to how you will deliver your services:

_____

_____

_____

_____

_____

THE TOOLSET #3 for
ESTABLISHING YOUR BRAND:
Identify & Prioritize Reputation-Brand Gaps

List the brand issues you want to work on. Before doing so, you might want to review Chapter 6, "Assessing Your Leadership Reputation." What gaps do you see between the reputation you have and the brand you want to build? Next, list ways you can learn and practice in key gap areas. Finally, prioritize your list and set specific goals and timetables to accomplish them. Here is an example:

REPUTATION-BRAND GAP:

Become a more engaging public speaker.

WAYS TO IMPROVE:

Use storytelling as a technique.

- Pay attention to how other speakers incorporate stories in their talks.
- Read material about how to use stories.
- Be on the lookout for events that are worth sharing.

GOALS AND TIMETABLE:

At our next monthly division meeting, I'll use one or two stories, not just data, to help convey our group's performance. I'll ask Jack to give me feedback.

COMMIT TO AN ACTION PLAN

Finally, having an action plan is essential. Practice may not make you perfect, but it will help you make progress. Once you have taken a close look at your current reputation, chosen your desired brand, and set goals for closing the gap, the best strategy for crafting your brand is to develop a specific plan. Many leaders work hard to get to the point at which it looks easy. Their comfort with leadership and with their brand is often the outcome of acquired skill and practice. Here are some key elements to consider in your action plan:

What new competencies might I need to develop to establish my brand?

What new knowledge will I need and how will I acquire that knowledge? What new skills, attitudes, and behaviors might I need to develop? How will I develop them?

How can my boss and my associates help me move toward my aspirational brand?

You can't do it alone. Your boss and colleagues are critical sources of feedback and support.

What metrics will I use to assess my progress?

How will I go about soliciting feedback on my progress, both on the work and how I am engaging with others?

"LIFE ISN'T ABOUT FINDING YOURSELF.
LIFE IS ABOUT CREATING YOURSELF."
- GEORGE BERNARD SHAW

KEY TAKEAWAYS in

ESTABLISHING YOUR LEADERSHIP BRAND

- ASSESS YOUR VALUES.

- IMAGINE YOUR DESIRED BRAND.

- IDENTIFY AND PRIORITIZE REPUTATION-BRAND GAPS.

- STRIVE FOR RELEVANCE AND AUTHENTICITY IN YOUR BRAND.

- REBRAND WHEN NECESSARY.

- PRACTICE, PRACTICE, PRACTICE.

- MEASURE PROGRESS AND RECALIBRATE.

CHAPTER FIFTEEN

COMMUNICATING YOUR VISION

Vision describes a direction and desired achievement, providing others with motivation, purpose, and a sense of clarity. More than a finite objective or a mission statement that describes a reason for being, a vision looks to the long-term future.

Whatever their vision may be, a key job for leaders is communicating and creating commitment to that vision. Without a clearly articulated and understood vision, employees may disagree about values and be unwilling to change or to be influenced in a particular direction. They may misunderstand the leader's intent or have trouble imagining the future state expressed in the vision. Effective communication of the vision is vital.

This chapter focuses on how to communicate vision effectively, even when your audience is resistant and even when you find yourself resistant to the direction. You'll learn how to help others understand the vision, remember it, be a part of it, and go on to share it themselves.

AT THE CONTROLS OF THE JUMBO JET'S FUTURE

In the high-flying competition between Airbus and Boeing to produce the preeminent commercial aircraft in the sky, there are no just-in-time changes in course. Plans and orders for the Super-Jumbo Airbus or Boeing's 787 Dreamliner are set years in advance.

So when Boeing found itself in a battle for the future with Airbus, company executives enlisted an unlikely ally: the very machinists Boeing had negotiated with in a combative 2014 contract extension. Only by being open with workers, Boeing leaders decided, could the organization achieve the buy-in it needed to prevail. Managers began sharing with them market information they had previously withheld.

"These are not the kinds of conversations that we've had with the workforce, all the way to the factory floor," CEO Ray Conner told investors, according to the Puget Sound Business *Journal.* "We're bringing the whole game to them so they can understand exactly how they fit into the entire system."

By clearly communicating a vision and being open with employees, company leaders appealed to the competitive mindset of a common organizational objective.

How might you be transparent and actively incorporate others into your vision?

THE POWER OF VISION

Leaders in today's organizations face issues of growth, change, customization, globalization, and technology that force them to create new pathways toward success and sustainability. But a newly blazed trail cannot itself create the necessary focus, tactics, and foresight to address these issues. As CCL's Kate Beatty and David Dinwoodie point out in *Becoming a Strategic Leader*, many organizations that falter in implementing their strategic vision have failed to effectively communicate their strategies. As a result, employees do not understand their role in implementing the organization's mission and strategy.

As the Boeing experience suggests, leaders can adopt tactics for coordinating messages and creating alignment among employees at every level. One effective tactic is to transmit strategic intent through a vision that clearly captures the organization's direction and defines its destination.

imaginable—creates an accessible picture of the future

inspiring—ignites desire and personal connection to values

realistic—is achievable, with focused direction and distinguishable outcomes

flexible—offers space to grow, adapt, and develop

clear—is easily communicated and understood

compelling—moves people to action

You may have heard the saying that a person who does not read is no better off than a person who cannot read. It's much the same with vision statements. Having a vision but not communicating it isn't much of an improvement over not having a vision at all.

As a leader, you're in the role of an early adopter. Your job is to communicate the vision to others in ways that will help them understand it, remember it, internalize it, and then go on to share it themselves. In this way, the vision becomes a bright lantern leading your organization on its path.

"IT'S KIND OF FUN TO DO THE IMPOSSIBLE."
- WALT DISNEY

Before we share our insights on communicating a vision, consider the ten behaviors listed below that typify a vision-driven leader; identify the three that you feel you are currently strongest in and the corresponding three that you feel are most in need of development.

STRENGTH	NEED	
☐	☐	Has a clear direction for the organization's future.
☐	☐	Connects his or her vision to real business outcomes.
☐	☐	Translates his or her vision into clear actions.
☐	☐	Shows passion for a vision of the future.
☐	☐	Stays focused on his or her vision.
☐	☐	Tells stories to capture the hearts and minds of followers.
☐	☐	Communicates his or her vision in a way that is meaningful and memorable.
☐	☐	Draws people together to share in his or her vision.
☐	☐	Repeats his or her vision to ensure that it is heard.
☐	☐	Takes advantage of multiple media to communicate vision.

Take a moment to reflect on how your perceived strengths and corresponding development needs in this area have played out in the past and currently. As you progress through this chapter, keep in mind how you might augment or leverage these approaches.

THE MINDSET for
COMMUNICATING YOUR VISION

One part of a leader's job is to create commitment to and alignment with the organization's picture of future success. But it's not enough just to say it. The vision has to be communicated with conviction and it has to be broadcast widely. Adopting these three mindsets will help.

CHANNEL YOUR PASSION

In order to inspire commitment to a vision, a leader needs to have an effective way to communicate it. Presumably, the leader supports the vision and can draw on his or her personal passion and professional commitment and credibility to be dynamic in presenting it to others.

NEVER STOP

You can never communicate too much. Treat every communication effort as though it is your most important attempt at getting the message out. People need time and opportunities to hear it, to separate the message from the noise of change. It takes more than one memo or speech to capture attention and build support.

CONNECT WITH HEAD, HEART, AND HANDS

When communicating a vision, we want people not only to understand the vision but also to remember it—and then to communicate it to others. The most effective route into memory varies from person to person, so take a diversified approach. In terms of an organizational vision, people need to understand it, believe in it, and follow it, so focus on appealing to the head, heart, and hands in your communication. Craft a communication that helps people to:

- UNDERSTAND THE VISION INTELLECTUALLY AND MENTALLY
- ACCEPT IT EMOTIONALLY AND PERSONALLY
- PUT IT INTO CONCRETE ACTION

'DON'T RAISE YOUR VOICE. IMPROVE YOUR ARGUMENT.'
- DESMOND TUTU

VISION DILEMMAS: CASCADING THE VISION

Communicating a vision is hard work. It's even harder when you are having to relay someone else's vision and inspire others. It's harder yet when you either don't fully understand or support that vision. Here are a few alternatives to consider in these less-than-ideal circumstances:

DON'T SAY: "This wasn't really my idea, but let's give it a try until there's something better."

INSTEAD SAY: "I don't know everything about this yet, but I'm committed to it."

DON'T SAY: "I had a different plan, but this is what they said, so let's get on with it."

INSTEAD SAY: "I'm fully on board with this, even though I'm still learning about it."

DON'T SAY: "I know this is stupid, but let's try to make the best of it, okay?"

INSTEAD SAY: "I'm learning along with you, so let's all be patient with any confusion or uncertainty."

THE SKILLSET for
COMMUNICATING YOUR VISION

Leaders who communicate the vision of their organization help employees see the importance of what they are doing. They communicate their passion to others, inspiring them and sparking them to take action. When you have gained skill in communicating your vision, you will be able to communicate a meaningful, ambitious vision for your organization that others will find motivating and attainable.

TELL A STORY

Stories give life to a vision and animate abstractions with common values and truths. By capturing both the heart and mind of the audience, stories establish common ground between the teller (the leader) and the audience (managers, employees, and other stakeholders). A story is a powerful tool for disseminating vision because it is easier for people to retell a story than a vision. In this way, stories create a ripple effect.

PREPARE AN ELEVATOR SPEECH

Not every situation lends itself to stories that take time to unwind, and that is where the 30- to 60-second elevator speech comes in. An elevator speech is a concise and convincing statement that communicates the vision in a carefully crafted sentence or two. Politicians, who thrive in a world of sound bites, are masters of the elevator speech that distills complicated positions into short, memorable statements. With practice and preparation, you can master it too. In a few minutes around the water cooler, in line at the cafeteria—or literally in an elevator—you can deliver a message that sounds natural and carries a sense of excitement.

"THE MOST COURAGEOUS ACT IS STILL TO THINK FOR YOURSELF. ALOUD."
- COCO CHANEL

ADVERTISE YOUR VISION

In our iPhone- and FaceTime-addicted world, actual face time sometimes seems a relic, as do posters and business card reminders. Our friends in marketing know better. The more channels you open, the better your chances of communicating, because not every method works with everybody. Your organization's vision should be out front on its website, but don't forget the tangible places: coffee mugs, T-shirts, letterhead, luggage tags, pencils, notepads—anything to keep your message out there. Repetition aids retention.

ENGAGE AN AUDIENCE OF ONE

Another effective strategy for communicating your vision is connecting with others in one-on-one conversations, which can be an extraordinarily effective way to communicate. These conversations give leaders concentrated opportunities to transmit information, receive feedback, build support, and create energy around the vision. A leader's skill at communicating a compelling and clear vision of the future is critical to fostering these deep connections.

MAKE IT PERSONAL

Leaders can inspire themselves and others by tapping into their personal visions. Someone with a personal vision of leadership that includes serving others so that more caring and appreciation can be brought into the world can inject the core of that vision into conversations about conflict, influence, power, strategy, empowerment, and many other leadership topics. Just a mention, in the context of personal relationships, can inform others and inspire them to think of the purpose and vision for their own leadership. Just as important, it keeps that particular leader inspired and aware of his or her own vision and invites rededication to it.

VOICES OF EXPERIENCE

TESLA'S VISION:
THE POWER OF SUNLIGHT

One of the many leadership lessons one can glean from Elon Musk, CEO of Tesla, is the power of transparency. In 2016, when the South African-born Musk unveiled "Part Deux" of his master plan to create a solar car, it was bold but not stunning. After all, that goal had been announced on Tesla's website ten years earlier.

"Starting a car company is idiocy," Musk wrote of his need for transparency, "and an electric car company is idiocy squared."

The need to communicate his end-stage vision—nothing less than producing a high-volume, self-driving, solar-powered car—was key. Unless the company could explain why it was producing in its first phase a low-volume, expensive car—about 100,000 units on the road as of 2016, with a base price of about $57,000—it would just be seen as a luxury car for the very rich.

But if Musk could explain Tesla's strategy, which was to use the profits for its pricey Roadster and Model S to fund research and development of an affordable electric car, both stakeholders and consumers would regard Tesla differently.

Beyond Tesla, Musk's ambition was to shake up the auto industry itself by inspiring technological innovation and new sales models, for example selling direct to customers instead of dealerships. Within its first decade, the company prompted General Motors to develop an electric car, and it had some success in removing historical barriers to the direct sales model.

Musk has been his own spokesman about what Tesla is competing against: "150 years and trillions of dollars spent on gasoline cars."

How might you challenge conventional wisdom and established ways of doing things with a clear, transparent vision that signals meaningful change?

THE TOOLSET for
COMMUNICATING YOUR VISION:
Bring Your Vision to Life

Details count when communicating your vision. Use the following criteria to craft a compelling message that engages head, heart, and hands.

Vision Elements	Definition	Ideas
INSPIRATIONAL IMAGERY	USE OF A DYNAMIC INTERACTION STYLE	
INCLUSIVE LANGUAGE	USE OF WE, OUR	
CLARITY	CLEAR, UNAMBIGUOUS STATEMENTS	
CHALLENGE	LANGUAGE AND IDEAS THAT MOTIVATE PEOPLE	
TASK AND GOAL SPECIFICATION	STRATEGIC AND TACTICAL PLANS	

KEY TAKEAWAYS in ESTABLISHING YOUR LEADERSHIP BRAND

CHANNEL YOUR PASSION.

KEEP COMMUNICATING—NEVER STOP.

CONNECT WITH HEAD, HEART, AND HANDS.

TELL STORIES.

MASTER THE ELEVATOR SPEECH.

USE MULTIPLE CHANNELS.

ENGAGE OTHERS ONE-ON-ONE.

CHAPTER SIXTEEN

SELLING YOURSELF
(WITHOUT SELLING OUT!)

A red sports car, just waiting to be raced at top speed. A meal at a Michelin 3-star restaurant, savoring every bite. A luxury hotel room on the top floor, where you open the curtains and take in the view.

Great things aren't there just to be admired. They have a job to do. Why should it be any different with people?

Unfortunately, individuals with a lot to offer are sometimes overlooked for their capabilities. The answer to avoiding this? It's promoting your work and career by generating personal visibility. You have a good product—now sell it.

In service of your work, your career, or your group, intentional and strategic self-promotion is nothing to shy away from. Quite the reverse. Many leaders expect visibility and recognition to result automatically from simply doing good work. Unfortunately, that is not the case.

This chapter shows you how you can benefit from self-promotion and maintain your integrity and authenticity. We help you reframe common beliefs that get in the way of effectively selling yourself, and we provide numerous strategies and activities that can become part of your repertoire and one of the keys to long-term success.

"BELIEVE IN YOURSELF AND WHAT YOU FEEL.
YOUR POWER WILL COME FROM THAT."
- MELISSA ETHERIDGE

PERSONAL BENEFITS OF STRATEGIC VISIBILITY

Self-promotion is a way to honestly leverage the accomplishments, strengths, and skills of people or groups. When we talk about being strategic in selling yourself, we mean that you are intentional in what you publicize and how. Leaders who effectively create visibility do so by being credible, consistent, and sincere. When approached with integrity, self-promotion builds the social capital needed to accomplish business outcomes.

First, let's consider the individual career benefits to you, the obvious ones being enhancing your pay and opportunities for promotion. There are other benefits to be gained that are more intrinsic in nature and just as valuable.

REWARDING OPPORTUNITIES. Gain new challenges, responsibilities, coworkers, and clients.

ENGAGEMENT. Acknowledgment can motivate you and sustain a commitment to the organization.

CONFIDENCE. The risk that accompanies promoting yourself can fuel confidence and also encourage you to capitalize on your strengths and develop new skills.

INCREASED SELF-WORTH. When others value your contributions and capabilities, it is strongly validating.

CREDIBILITY. When your reputation matches your accomplishments, you gain trust.

INFLUENCE. Negotiating for scarce resources, generating support, staying in the know, influencing decisions—these are all expectations of leaders. When others have confidence in your abilities, you can better meet these expectations.

BENEFITS FOR OTHERS

SELF-PROMOTION ISN'T ONLY ABOUT YOURSELF. It's also about your obligations to others. When it comes to touting their work, leaders should think beyond their personal interests.

DIRECT REPORTS. Advocating and creating opportunities for your direct reports demonstrates that you respect the talent in your department and want others to do the same.

BOSS. When you update your boss about a value added or a successful negotiation, you enable an accurate view of people's talents, generating visibility for the boss's group.

GROUP. Promoting yourself helps enroll others in the energy of the work. You can foster pride in the group's work by sharing recognition, visibility, and opportunities to learn.

ORGANIZATION. The organization deserves the best information and ideas that are generated by its people. Only by sharing information about skills and accomplishments can you help the organization fully leverage opportunities for collaboration, contributions, and advancement—including your own.

Now that you have a better idea of what we are (and aren't) talking about when we say "selling yourself," consider the ten behaviors listed below that typify a leader skilled at authentic self-promotion; identify the three that you feel you are currently strongest in and the corresponding three that you feel are most in need of development.

STRENGTH	NEED	
☐	☐	Intentionally communicates capabilities and accomplishments.
☐	☐	Embraces self-promotion as part of being an effective leader.
☐	☐	Promotes self in an authentic manner.
☐	☐	Promotes self for the benefit of others.
☐	☐	Promotes self to a variety of stakeholders.
☐	☐	Strikes a balance between bragging and being overly modest.
☐	☐	Invites others into his or her work.
☐	☐	Listens to audience and identifies shared needs.
☐	☐	Creates or seizes opportunities for visibility.
☐	☐	Shares credit and gives others an opportunity to be recognized.

Take a moment to reflect on how your perceived strengths and corresponding development needs in this area have played out in the past and currently. As you progress through this chapter, keep in mind how you might augment or leverage these approaches.

VOICES OF EXPERIENCE

CHRISTIANE AMANPOUR: FROM "TEA BOY" TO CHIEF INTERNATIONAL CORRESPONDENT AT CNN

She is one of the most influential journalists on the world scene, dispatched to so many trouble spots that soldiers jokingly track her movements to guess where they will deploy next.

But when Christiane Amanpour arrived in 1983 at the fledgling cable network CNN, she had nothing but a bicycle, $100 in her pocket, and a lofty idea.

"I was really just the tea boy, or the equivalent thereof, to begin with," she once told historian Anthony Fellow. "But I quickly announced, innocently but very ambitiously, that I wanted to be, I was going to be, a foreign correspondent."

The ensuing arc of Amanpour's career is a textbook example of making your own luck—in other words, creating a personal brand and then selling it. Iranian-born and English-educated, Amanpour promoted her internationalist identity, bilingualism, and knowledge of world affairs to communicate her capabilities and vision for her future role.

She climbed the ladder rung by rung, beginning by conducting person-on-the-street "vox pop" interviews with ordinary people. "Nothing was too paltry," she said. But by combining promotion of her genuine abilities, consistent performance, and cohesive branding, Amanpour eventually promoted herself into the role she aspired to all along.

How might you combine Amanpour's potent blend of authenticity and ambition to shape the future you envision for your career?

THE MINDSET of the
AUTHENTIC
SELF-PROMOTING LEADER

Many leaders aren't comfortable with the concept and practice of self-promotion. It is often viewed with derision—as a personal public-relations campaign, a way of shouting "Look at me! I'm the best!" Even leaders who see the value of self-promotion are often unsure how to proceed.

Many of us have beliefs or mindsets that get in the way of effective self-promotion. As a result, many talented managers avoid promoting themselves, their work, and their groups. Unfortunately, they and their organizations are missing out on the benefits of greater visibility.

To overcome your hesitancy or aversion, it is helpful to understand common barriers to effective self-promotion. We call these limiting beliefs. If you can find a new perspective, or reframe your belief, you'll find that self-promotion will become more natural and more effective.

LIMITING BELIEF: Accomplishments should speak for themselves.

REFRAMED: A lot of good work falls under the radar.

Many people believe they shouldn't have to promote themselves because good work will speak for itself. Or they believe that meeting the requirements of the job ("I'm just doing my job. What is there to promote?") will provide sufficient visibility. Unfortunately, this is not true. Many managers are surprised to find that bosses, peers, and direct reports do not recognize their skills and contributions. It is your job to let people know about your work, why it is important, and how it benefits others.

Never assume that you will be noticed, given credit, or rewarded for your accomplishments if you don't share them. Nor should you assume the word-of-mouth grapevine will work in your favor. You need to communicate with all of your stakeholders.

LIMITING BELIEF: Productivity trumps promoting.

REFRAMED: Promoting is productive.

Promoting yourself and your group is part of your job. If you want to be truly productive, you need to shift your mental model away from seeing self-promotion as a waste of time. Instead, look at it as a way to sell yourself as a resource to the organization. Your productivity will not be jeopardized; in fact, it will improve when you have the information and the relationships to get the resources, information, and support you need.

LIMITING BELIEF: Senior management doesn't want to hear about me.

REFRAMED: Senior management appreciates information and talent.

Here again, effective self-promotion isn't just about you but also about your leadership role. Although senior managers do not need excruciating detail about you and your current task, they do want to know that you are engaged in your work and in the goals of the organization.

Have a clear statement in mind—a promotional sound bite—about a key project or component of your work. If you're asked about your work, you can take advantage of the moment to demonstrate your credibility as a communicator and a leader. For instance, if someone asks, "How is your project?" don't limit your response to "It's fine" or "We're really busy." Instead say, "The project is great," and then briefly describe what you've done so far and how it's making a difference.

'COMMITMENT IS NOT A WORD. IT IS AN ACT.'
- JEAN-PAUL SARTRE

THE SWEET SPOT

Self-promotion is necessary to business success, but like most behaviors, it can be overdone or underdone to your detriment. To develop strong, effective self-promotional skills, leaders need to learn the difference between over-the-top, obnoxious bragging and the kind of exaggerated modesty that is equally dishonest in its own way and results in good work being overlooked.

To find the sweet spot, stay focused on the value of the work. Take yourself out of the equation . . . even though you will gain and benefit. By focusing on the work itself, you will not go overboard with bragging, nor will your hesitancy to be in the spotlight become a liability.

QUIZ: WHAT'S YOUR PROMOTIONAL PERSONALITY?

Can you spot your behaviors and reactions in one of the descriptions below?

Schmoozer. You are highly social and know everybody. You like to see and be seen, particularly with "the right people."

Your challenge: Make sure that you are not perceived as a phony with little substance and a big agenda; your interactions should be meaningful and genuine with everybody.

New mindset: Self-promotion should be targeted, intentional, and sincere.

. . . .

Worker. You are highly competent, work oriented, and productive. You view social activities, networking, and self-promotion as time wasters.

Your challenge: Expand your view beyond the task and take a broader view; see how connections enable you to have stronger impact.

New mindset: Self-promotion contributes to workplace effectiveness.

. . . .

Anti-braggart. You see self-promotion as boastful and obnoxious and will go to extremes not to be perceived that way. Overly modest, you often deflect praise and are quick to take blame.

Your challenge: Ensure that your skills and your work are viewed and valued accurately by others; stop downplaying your contributions.

New mindset: There's a difference between bragging and authentic self-promotion.

. . . .

Selective marketer. You know the value of self-promotion and have had some positive experiences as a result of touting your work, your group, and your talent. Even so, you are unsure of how to consistently or strategically market yourself without overdoing it.

Your challenge: Integrate self-promotion into your routine work and communication so that it is appropriate, useful, and consistent.

New mindset: Self-promotion is an ongoing leadership task, not an occasional activity.

THE SKILLSET for
AUTHENTIC SELF-PROMOTION

The first rule of getting yourself noticed may seem like a no-brainer: There have to be people around! Second, you need to provide them with something worthy of their attention. With that in mind, the tips in this chapter are divided into two categories: first, gathering your audience; and, second, putting on a show.

GATHER YOUR AUDIENCE

Connecting with others addresses strategies and tactics that help you build your network, create relationships, and gain visibility in the organization. Developing yourself focuses on skills and behaviors that are useful in your efforts to promote yourself.

CROSS-POLLINATE. Sometimes the best ideas come from unexpected sources. Allow more people to be part of your team, initiative, or problem-solving process. You can draw on their information, expertise, and experience.

EXTEND AN INVITATION. Invite people from other areas of the business to sit in on a meeting to give a fresh perspective. An "outsider" may have useful ideas and information to share, or may simply stimulate good discussion. You may also discover common concerns and find ways to work together or share resources.

> "IT'S NOT BRAGGING IF YOU CAN BACK IT UP."
> - MUHAMMAD ALI

INVOLVE SENIOR PEOPLE. To get noticed and implemented, many good concepts need a person with formal authority or a high degree of influence. Ask seasoned or senior people for their insights and opinions. Once they've given their input, you have a good reason to keep them informed.

ASK FOR HELP. One of the simplest and often overlooked ways of making useful connections is to ask for help. By asking for other people's assistance, you naturally have to describe your work. They may not have known of your involvement in a project, and this gives you a sincere way to talk about your work.

CONNECT WITH A NEED. Consider your audience and find ways to connect with their needs. Listen to people's concerns and suggestions. What are you doing that affects them or benefits them? Do you have a shared need? Promoting yourself can be a win-win when you understand others' points of view.

PUT ON A SHOW

In addition to connecting to others, practice ethical self-promotion by engaging in these practices at the right time and the right place. The following actions lend themselves to making yourself more visible to the organization.

FIND THE FORUM. Take opportunities in public forums (group or staff meetings) to diplomatically report on accomplishments, achievements, milestones, and successes you are genuinely proud of.

STEP INTO THE SPOTLIGHT. Take on challenging work assignments or high-visibility projects. If the project is highly visible, you have a better chance of getting noticed. To make your projects visible to management, ask for opportunities to present what you've done to specific groups that can benefit.

CHOOSE—AND USE—YOUR EVENTS. You don't need to attend every employee function, and you certainly don't need to talk to everyone every time. Identify one or two people you would like to meet or speak with. An easy approach is to attend corporate social events that you are genuinely interested in. For example, if your corporation holds a charity event, you may enjoy the chance to give to your community. But you'll also benefit from the interaction with people outside your immediate work group.

COME UP WITH YOUR OWN EVENT. Host a speaker and invite people from other departments to attend. Propose an award for an important achievement, manage the process, and be the one to present the honors. Set up a lunch group with one or two other people, with the rule that each person must bring someone else for the group to get to know.

'DISCIPLINING YOURSELF TO DO WHAT YOU KNOW IS RIGHT AND IMPORTANT, ALTHOUGH DIFFICULT, IS THE HIGH ROAD TO PRIDE, SELF-ESTEEM, AND PERSONAL SATISFACTION.'
- MARGARET THATCHER

THE TOOLSET for
AUTHENTIC SELF-PROMOTION:
Setting Up Your Promotional Tour

Self-promotion can definitely be done in the moment, but it often involves some planned effort. Take a moment to identify a particular challenge or opportunity that's looming ahead of you, where some strategic efforts at self-promotion will help influence the outcomes you're seeking. Then fill out the following chart:

Audience	Why	Desired Outcome	When	How

KEY TAKEAWAYS in
SELLING YOURSELF
(WITHOUT SELLING OUT!)

REFRAME LIMITING BELIEFS ABOUT SELF-PROMOTION.

STRIKE A BALANCE BETWEEN BRAGGING AND BEING OVERLY MODEST.

PROMOTE IN AN AUTHENTIC MANNER

PROMOTE FOR THE GOOD OF YOURSELF AND OTHERS.

GATHER YOUR AUDIENCE.

PICK THE RIGHT TIME AND PLACE FOR PROMOTIONAL ACTIVITIES.

ENGAGE IN PLANNED, PROACTIVE PROMOTIONAL EFFORTS.

CHAPTER SEVENTEEN

BUILDING AND MAINTAINING TRUST

For organizations awash in change, transition is no longer a periodic event. It's the only event.

Economic, political, technological, cultural, and societal upheavals all contribute to the pace and complexity of change. The change may come from within, such as a downsizing, expansion, or merger. But more likely it will be driven by external factors, such as holding the lead in a market or struggling to gain one.

The challenge of leading organizations through change goes beyond setting strategy, making plans, and implementing the structures and processes of change. Often, the real struggle lies in weathering wave upon wave of recovery, revitalization, and recommitment—an emotional typhoon for teams.

Those steering the ship must focus simultaneously on keeping the business on course and on effective leadership of the crew. When the people side of that equation loses out, the issue often comes down to one factor: loss of trust.

Trust is never something to take for granted, but circumstances of change and upheaval pose some of the most serious threats to building and maintaining trust. This chapter focuses on how to respond to the human toll of rapid change and keep trust intact.

Ignoring this dynamic poses two risks. First, it may undermine the organization's structural and strategic goals because there is lack of buy-in and commitment from employees. Second, it can destabilize the organization's culture, eroding values that engender dedication in the first place. Loyalty and trust give way to insecurity and fear, while productivity and enthusiasm are displaced by withdrawal and skepticism.

Trust and authenticity are leadership qualities that go hand-in-hand and little is possible without them. Building authenticity into your leadership requires that you see both yourself and others as complex, whole people—emotions included. This perspective takes into account that, during times of change, you and everyone else in the organization are collectively steering a course through the events that surround you, but each of you is navigating separately in the context of your own life, and no one has the same set of circumstances.

As a leader, your ability to appreciate and bear that complexity in mind is important for you to be effective in extraordinary times. Leading with authenticity flows from self-knowledge: awareness of your own emotions, expectations, struggles, motivations, preferences, frustrations, contradictions. How do we achieve that self-awareness? Experience, action, feedback, reflection.

People look for leaders who can appreciate their vulnerability and inspire them, understand them, support them, and guide them through the looming chaos. Leaders meet those needs by being genuine and vulnerable, traits that are themselves powerful learning tools.

Leading with authenticity during transition isn't a checklist or a series of buzzwords. It's about

- LOOKING INWARD

- SEEING HOW YOUR PERSONALITY, BEHAVIOR, AND EMOTIONS PLAY OUT AS YOU TAKE A LEADERSHIP ROLE

- UNDERSTANDING THE DYNAMICS OF CHANGE AND TRANSITION

- DISCOVERING OPENNESS AND VULNERABILITY

- VALUING AND BUILDING TRUST

These are big concepts. We will examine specific behaviors that help leaders make them real. Before we continue, consider the ten behaviors listed below that typify a leader who builds and maintains trust; identify the three that you feel you are currently strongest in and the corresponding three that you feel are most in need of development.

STRENGTH	NEED	
☐	☐	Understands the role of trust in leading change and transition.
☐	☐	Makes efforts to create trust rooted in authentic behaviors.
☐	☐	Uses a diverse set of behaviors to build trust.
☐	☐	Emphasizes the right behaviors at the right time to reinforce trust.
☐	☐	Balances catalyzing change with coping with transition.
☐	☐	Balances sense of urgency with realistic patience.
☐	☐	Balances toughness with empathy.
☐	☐	Balances optimism with realism and openness.
☐	☐	Balances self-reliance with trusting others.
☐	☐	Balances capitalizing on strengths with going against the grain.

Take a moment to reflect on how your perceived strengths and corresponding development needs in this area have played out in the past and currently. As you progress through this chapter, keep in mind how you might augment or leverage these approaches.

SEEKING TRUST AMID CHANGE:
AUSTRALIA'S MACCAS AND ANTI-MACCAS

As one of the largest employers on the continent, McDonald's Australia—popularly known as "Maccas"—faced challenges as supersized as its once competitive dominance.

Sales were falling. "Anti-Macca" activists staged flashmob protests. Meanwhile, the company's own constituents were not "lovin' it." Customers disliked an all-day breakfast menu. Suppliers disliked a "cage-free" egg initiative. Franchise owners disliked a companywide employee pay raise.

That's when the company took several counterintuitive steps. One was to acknowledge its unpopularity with a TV ad campaign. "How very un-McDonald's," the ads confided. "Everything you thought we were, we're not."

Another tactic was an effort to be up front about its ingredients. An iPhone app, TrackMyMaccas, used QR codes to "track the ingredients in the actual food you just bought" through a combination of GPS, image recognition, and date-time stamps to pinpoint the origin of a Big Mac's beef, bun, cheese, pickles, and other ingredients.

The company promoted its Junior Sports Grants to ally itself with a healthy image for youth, and it sought to give Australians more choice with computer screens allowing patrons to "make your own burger."

None of these choices by the fast-food giant placated ardent anti-Maccas, who continued to protest new stores being built. But McDonald's, by recognizing changing tastes, attempted to demonstrate to its customer base that it listened to and acknowledged criticism, sought transparency, and shared community values.

How might you and your organization respond to your critics in a way that demonstrates empathy and fosters trust?

THE MINDSET of
BUILDING AND MAINTAINING TRUST

Change and transition are separate but related. Change is the event; transition represents the psychological and emotional adaptation to it. At work, as well as in our personal lives, adaptation is how we let go of the old and accept the new.

Wise leaders recognize that when change is not going well, it is likely because people are stuck in some part of the transition and are not ready to let go. After all, change is risky. There is a drop in competency and comfort at first, which is the steep end of the learning curve.

Leaders who attack the problem only on the structural side—reiterating the plans and rationale, pushing the data or measurements—fail to resolve the problem of transition. An additional part of your leadership task is to connect to the personal and the emotional fallout of change, which is the hard work of letting go, learning, and rebuilding.

To help you remain authentic in extraordinary times and build trust against a backdrop of continuous change, we've identified three initial steps.

EXAMINE YOUR MENTAL MODELS

We all have habitual patterns of thinking, perceiving, and behaving. When you are aware of these patterns, you can make conscious choices about how to operate as a leader. Assumptions left unexamined cause you to repeat patterns that may not serve you well during challenging times.

UNDERSTAND THAT CHANGE DOES NOT EQUAL TRANSITION

Leaders need to realize that transition is a process often fraught with self-doubt and uncertainty. People may be reluctant to accept the reality that something is ending. When you or someone in the organization is struggling with change, acknowledge transition by exploring what has been lost and what is impeding adaptation.

IMPROVE YOUR ABILITY TO LEARN

Most of what you need to know about leading through transition you will learn from experience. If you can learn and adapt (and help others to do so), not only will you recover from change and loss but you will in fact thrive. By becoming a more versatile learner, you increase your capacity to cope, adapt, and move on to what's next.

"EARN TRUST, EARN TRUST, EARN TRUST.
THEN YOU CAN WORRY ABOUT THE REST."
- SETH GODIN

THE TOOLSET for
BUILDING AND MAINTAINING TRUST:
"The Trust Wheel"

We often use the image of a bicycle wheel to describe the leadership competencies that are important during times of transition. On a bicycle wheel, each spoke needs to be tightened or loosened to the right tension. Otherwise, there will be strain on the other spokes, pulling the wheel out of alignment and making the bike much more difficult to ride. Avid cyclists keep their bikes rolling at top performance by "truing" their wheels— adjusting the tension of the spokes—as part of their routine bicycle maintenance.

Imagine, now, a wheel that has trust as its hub. Radiating out from that hub are the spokes, which represent twelve competencies that support authentic, effective leadership in times of transition. Six spokes represent structural competencies; the other six represent people-related (or transition) competencies. Any of the twelve competencies can be overdone, underdone, or held in a positive, dynamic balance (as the spokes on a bicycle wheel are set in a balanced tension). If a leader neglects or devotes an overabundance of energy to any one element, he or she runs the risk of skewing the opposite, pushing the wheel out of true, and creating undue strain on the trust needed to lead effectively during extraordinary times.

SETTING THINGS ARIGHT

It's easy to slide off kilter—in both cycling and leadership. But while a cyclist can stop riding to fix a wheel, leaders have no choice but to keep moving forward even as changes swirl around them. Adding to their difficulty is the fact that experience and its lessons are coupled with personal preferences to exaggerate or downplay various leadership practices. This often pushes leaders toward emphasizing a select number of leadership competencies—usually the ones that they have been schooled in, the ones organizations reinforce and reward.

Those competencies often fall on the structural side of change management. When leaders pay less attention to the people side of change, the tension between the two sides of the wheel can slip out of balance and negatively impact their effectiveness, how they are perceived, and the trust they require to guide people through the phases of transition.

Often, people are hypersensitive during times of stress and threat. Using our metaphor of the bicycle wheel, people won't likely say, "You have a few spokes that need tuning," when they experience a ride on your bicycle. They are more likely to generalize and say, "Your bike is broken." In the same way, people can make sweeping judgments about authenticity and genuineness based on small cues and data.

"TRUST HAS TO BE EARNED,
AND SHOULD COME ONLY AFTER THE PASSAGE OF TIME."
- ARTHUR ASHE

To lead with authenticity, effective managers develop new behaviors and find appropriate ways to work with the structural and the people sides of change. They don't swing wildly from one end to the other. By learning about the twelve change-related leadership competencies and how they relate to each other, managers and executives can tease out adjustments to maintain or improve their level of trust and effectiveness as situations change.

Here are the twelve competencies that comprise the spokes in the wheel:

- Catalyzing change is championing an initiative or significant change.
- Coping with transition recognizes the personal and emotional elements of change.
- Sense of urgency involves taking action quickly when necessary to keep things rolling.
- Realistic patience involves knowing when and how to slow the pace to allow people to adapt.
- Being tough is the ability to make difficult decisions with neither hesitation nor second-guessing.
- Being empathetic requires consideration of others' perspectives when making decisions.
- Optimism is the ability to see the positive potential of any challenge.
- Realism and openness denotes a grounded perspective and a willingness to not gloss over problems.
- Self-reliance involves a willingness to take a lead role and do something yourself when necessary.
- Trusting others means being comfortable with allowing others to do their parts of a task or project.
- Capitalizing on strengths entails knowing your strengths and confidently applying them.
- Going against the grain entails a willingness to learn and try new things, even when hard or painful.

TAKE THE WHEEL

Now plot your self-ratings on the accompanying wheel. For each of the twelve competencies, mark a dot along the spoke that best indicates your typical leadership behavior.

The **BLACK** line represents behavior that is just about right.

The **GRAY** area is overdoing a competency.

The **WHITE** area is underdoing it.

Transition Leadership Wheel

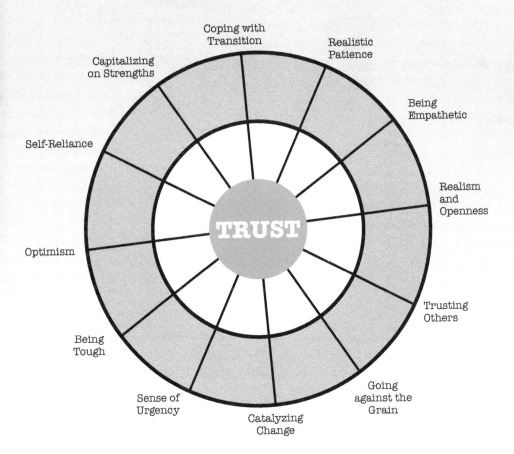

This exercise will give you a fairly accurate representation of whether your leadership is balanced. Do you see tension between opposing spokes? Are some of your mental models about leadership conducive to leading in the constant change of contemporary organizational life?

Another useful exercise is to plot your self-ratings in one color and the perceptions you think others have of you in another color. The differences between the two perspectives can be informative. Of course, the real test would be to take these reflections and share them with a trusted colleague.

You can also use the wheel to plot the leadership behaviors valued by your organization. If a leader performed only the behaviors rewarded by the organization, what would that profile look like? Comparing that profile to your self-ratings may help you recognize where your personal values and beliefs correspond or collide with those of your organization.

"THE DAY SOLDIERS STOP BRINGING YOU THEIR PROBLEMS IS THE DAY YOU HAVE STOPPED LEADING THEM. THEY HAVE EITHER LOST CONFIDENCE THAT YOU CAN HELP THEM OR CONCLUDED THAT YOU DO NOT CARE. EITHER CASE IS A FAILURE OF LEADERSHIP."
 - COLIN POWELL

THE SKILLSET for
BUILDING AND MAINTAINING TRUST

You may have noticed in completing the wheel that each of these capabilities is important; at the same time there are inherent conflicts between and paradoxes among them. Why is that?

It's complicated. It's simple.

In the face of change and turmoil, people look for leaders who are simultaneously strong and vulnerable, heroic and open, demanding and compassionate. Managing those opposing demands can feel impossible. Finding the right behaviors, tone, and style requires blending characteristics that appear paradoxical but nonetheless coexist and complement one another. The "right" balance varies by situation and point in time.

In times of transition, be alert to signs that your leadership balance is off-center. This is when authentic leaders recalibrate so that none of these twelve competencies are overly exaggerated or overly downplayed and trust can be maintained.

Consider these tips in relation to when you may be likely to experience an imbalance in your approach:

CATALYZING CHANGE VERSUS COPING WITH TRANSITION

Be genuine. Make more of yourself available. Let people see who you are in times of stress, crisis, and change, when sensitivities are heightened. Let down the managerial guard you have kept over the years and be real with people. You may feel vulnerable, but masking this rarely fools people and your self-protective efforts will only erode trust.

URGENCY VERSUS PATIENCE

Don't squash resistance. Instead, process it and look for useful information in the way people resist change and transition. The nature of resistance can inform you about what people value and what they are afraid of losing. That needs to be acknowledged rather than swept aside.

TOUGHNESS VERSUS EMPATHY

Pay attention to unintended consequences. Always ask what the fallout might be from any decision. Negative consequences must be weighed against positive long-term impact. Dilemmas reign supreme during transitions because no single answer can satisfy all of the complexities of organizational problems. Informed choices, even trade-offs, will at least be better understood by those affected.

REALISM VERSUS OPTIMISM

Seek to understand obstacles from other perspectives. Don't overdo optimism and self-confidence to the point of not recognizing genuine barriers or mistakes. Use candor to cultivate trust and respect. Telling the truth is a springboard for creative strategies and renewed energy.

SELF-RELIANCE VERSUS INTERDEPENDENCE

Open up. Seek out a few trusted colleagues with whom you feel safe discussing your work and your leadership role. Build a network of peers with whom you can go offline and talk. Use these connections to raise unresolved issues or to vent some of your personal frustrations. There is power in learning to be situationally vulnerable about fears, concerns, and mistakes. Don't play superhero.

CAPITALIZING STRENGTHS VERSUS GOING AGAINST THE GRAIN

Encourage new thinking. Honor and reward those willing to put time and energy into novel solutions—even when their attempts might be incremental, expansive, tried before, rule challenging, or just plain illogical. Question people respectfully with the goal of mining any and all aspects of their ideas. Are there pieces, concepts, or perspectives that may shed new light on the issues?

KEY TAKEAWAYS in
BUILDING AND MAINTAINING TRUST

RECOGNIZE the **DIFFERENCE** BETWEEN CHANGE AND TRANSITION.

BALANCE CATALYZING CHANGE WITH COPING WITH TRANSITION.

BALANCE SENSE of **URGENCY** WITH REALISTIC PATIENCE.

BALANCE BEING TOUGH WITH BEING EMPATHIC.

BALANCE OPTIMISM WITH REALISM AND OPENNESS.

BALANCE SELF-RELIANCE WITH TRUSTING OTHERS.

BALANCE CAPITALIZING ON STRENGTHS WITH GOING AGAINST THE GRAIN.

CHAPTER EIGHTEEN

LEVERAGING YOUR NETWORK

Picture a forest where only one kind of tree grows, and every one of the trees was planted at the same time. No moss. No underbrush. No canopy. Now imagine that a drought dries up the soil and the insects along with it. Birds go silent. Bees disappear. With no cross-pollination, the buds shrivel and the roots wither. Before long . . .

Most of us understand the idea of biodiversity, the necessary interdependence of ecosystems. And if leadership is a social activity, as we've shown, then it, too, is a kind of ecosystem that thrives on diversity. Instead of soil, roots, and several species of animal life, it's built on interlocking relationships that sustain knowledge, ability, and wisdom.

Think of your leadership network, the connections you build, as an ecosystem that affects how you share and receive new ideas. Networks also build social capital, interdisciplinary collaboration, and cross-functional integration. Formal channels are often insufficient mechanisms for coordination and cooperation. Networks are a means of cross-pollination that allow leaders to locate resources and information outside their routine interactions. Personal connections formed through networks build coalitions, influence others, and reconcile goals that would otherwise have business units working at cross purposes.

On the flip side of this, CCL research identifies patterns of leaders who:

- PLATEAU PREMATURELY AND ARE DEMOTED OR FIRED.
- SHOW DIFFICULTY BUILDING AND LEADING TEAMS.
- HAVE TROUBLED INTERPERSONAL RELATIONSHIPS.
- FAIL TO ADAPT TO AND LEAD CHANGE.
- MISS BUSINESS OPPORTUNITIES.
- HAVE TOO NARROW A FUNCTIONAL ORIENTATION.

What is at the root of many of these problems? Leaders' networks—or lack thereof.

Networks are at the heart of creating social capital for your future. With an accurate network perspective and the accompanying skills, you can strategically invest in your personal networks and build the influence that is needed to pursue your vision and goals at each stage of your career. And when the unexpected occurs and you need to marshal resources and support, networks can be indispensable.

NETWORK IS A VERB

Conventional wisdom often places networking in the context of looking for a new job, chatting at parties and events, or working in sales. That's a nice capability to have in those situations, but leadership networking is not principally concerned with collecting business cards or schmoozing. Where it is an essential skill is in the day-to-day work of leading and making alliances in service of other people—customers, clients, constituents, peers, bosses, and employees—all to advance the organization.

Leaders who create strong, broad-based networks:

- INCREASE EFFECTIVENESS BY DEEPENING COMMUNICATION CHANNELS BETWEEN INDIVIDUALS AND GROUPS.
- REMOVE POLITICAL ROADBLOCKS BY BRIDGING DISTANCES THAT SEPARATE BUSINESS UNITS.
- OPEN UP NEW OPPORTUNITIES AND UNCOVER IDEAS BY "CROSS-POLLINATING" WITH OTHERS.
- STRENGTHEN THEIR POWER BASE BY BOTH ACCEPTING AND DELIVERING SUPPORT WHEN NEEDED.
- GAIN EXPOSURE ACROSS THEIR ORGANIZATIONS BY HIGHLIGHTING INDIVIDUAL EFFORTS WITHIN THEIR GROUPS.

Some managers in leadership roles are ambivalent about or even averse to the idea of networking, regarding it as tedious or self-serving. But becoming a more effective leader requires developing relationships with others. If managers set aside conventional notions of top-down leadership, the reality is that they can take networking and other related interpersonal skills, such as political savvy and getting support for your vision, to a higher level.

"SOMETIMES, IDEALISTIC PEOPLE ARE PUT OFF THE WHOLE BUSINESS OF NETWORKING AS SOMETHING TAINTED BY FLATTERY AND THE PURSUIT OF SELFISH ADVANTAGE. BUT VIRTUE IN OBSCURITY IS REWARDED ONLY IN HEAVEN. TO SUCCEED IN THIS WORLD, YOU HAVE TO BE KNOWN TO PEOPLE."
— SONIA SOTOMAYOR

Before we delve into the mindset, skillset, and toolset for leveraging your network, consider the ten behaviors listed below that typify a network-savvy leader; identify the three that you feel you are currently strongest in and the corresponding three that you feel are most in need of development.

STRENGTH	NEED	
☐	☐	Has a positive view of networking.
☐	☐	Actively engages in networking activities.
☐	☐	Maintains relationships within existing network.
☐	☐	Seeks out new relationships as needs and circumstances change.
☐	☐	Understands how to draw upon network relationships.
☐	☐	Approaches network relationships as a two-way street.
☐	☐	Is concerned with meeting others' needs as well as having own needs met.
☐	☐	Leverages network to both solve problems and create opportunities.
☐	☐	Regards networking activities as transcending organizational, geographic, or other barriers.
☐	☐	Is direct and transparent in approach to networking with others.

Take a moment to reflect on how your perceived strengths and corresponding development needs in this area have played out in the past and currently. As you progress through this chapter, keep in mind how you might augment or leverage these approaches.

NETWORKING A REVERSE DISASTER:
THE ICE BUCKET CHALLENGE

In the United States, during the heat of August 2014, thousands of people were dumping buckets of ice water on their heads. The reason: In one of the most successful fund-raising campaigns in history, participants raised $115 million for medical research into ALS, a fatal disease of the brain and spinal cord.

And even stranger than the phenomenon of ice-drenched people sharing videos of themselves on social media, the money was largely unsolicited, and the campaign began as a spontaneous instance of networking on a scale previously seen only in response to disasters. But this was a disaster in reverse.

Eventually known as the Ice Bucket Challenge, the idea began as a small gesture of support among friends of a person suffering from ALS. Soon it began to spread from state to state and coast to coast, with sports stars, entertainers, even former presidents challenging each other to raise money for the cause.

The phenomenon had its critics, who called it everything from "impulse charity"—in which donors lacked true commitment—to "funding cannibalism," which risked draining potential donations to research on more widespread diseases such as cancer or Alzheimer's.

Yet the campaign illustrated the immense power of networks to get results that could otherwise have taken years to achieve. The direct outcome was that within a year after the Ice Bucket Challenge, research scientists at Johns Hopkins leveraged the resources generated to advance experiments that isolated the gene that causes ALS, with an eye toward halting the progressive disease.

How might you harness the power of your (and, by association, others') networks to create a ripple effect of positive change?

THE MINDSET of the
NETWORKING LEADER

Leaders may face the temptation to build expansive networks, but a large network isn't necessarily a good network. The demands of large networks can be draining—and still not provide access to the information, resources, and relationships that matter most to be effective. To build an effective network, shift your mindset from focusing on the number of people to paying attention to quality and structure.

Have a look at the two networks depicted on the next page. Which do you think provides more opportunities for new ideas or influence?

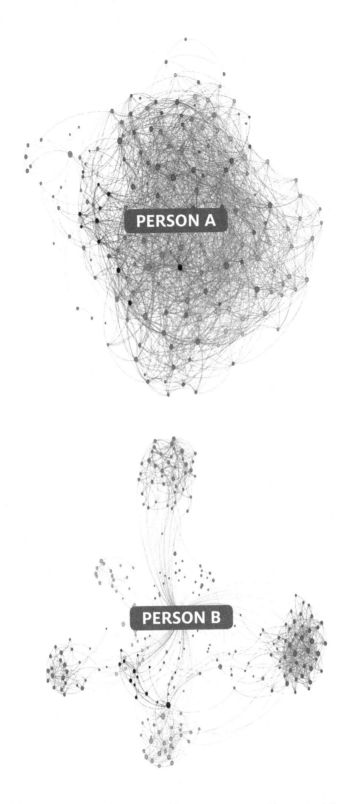

PERSON A

PERSON B

Many people choose the image on the top, but in fact, the one on the bottom offers greater opportunities. Here are three elements that distinguish that network and should be part of your focus in network building.

GOOD NETWORKS ARE OPEN

Open networks are those where the people you know are not all connected to each other. This creates what is called structural diversity in a leader's network. Leaders with open networks are more likely to hear new information before others. They are better able to merge dissimilar ideas and capitalize on opportunities that require this integration. They tend to perform better, are promoted more rapidly, enjoy greater career mobility, and adapt to change more effectively.

GOOD NETWORKS ARE DIVERSE

Connections that cross critical boundaries in the organization provide additional diversity—and many of the same advantages of open networks. Much of the work of leadership involves working across vertical, horizontal, stakeholder, demographic, and geographic boundaries for group and organizational success. An individual leader's network connections form the bridges that span these boundaries and allow for collective action.

GOOD NETWORKS ARE DEEP

Leaders who build deep, quality relationships with others are able to exchange information, resources, and skills with people from different backgrounds. These deep relationships provide valuable perspective and resources, including social support and camaraderie in the workplace. Building high-quality relationships with others is estimated to be four times the predictor of performance compared to other network predictors.

FIVE NETWORKING MYTHS

The following statements are actually false:

1. DEVELOPING STRATEGIC RELATIONSHIPS IS INSINCERE AND MANIPULATIVE.

2. PEOPLE BUILD AND USE THEIR NETWORKS ONLY TO GET AHEAD.

3. NETWORKING IS NOT REAL WORK, SO LEADERS SHOULDN'T BUILD IN TIME FOR IT.

4. THE GOAL IS TO INCREASE THE NUMBER OF BUSINESS CARDS IN YOUR POCKET, CONTACTS IN OUTLOOK, CONNECTIONS ON LINKEDIN, OR TWITTER FOLLOWERS.

5. YOU NEED A CERTAIN PERSONALITY TO SUCCEED IN NETWORKING.

How might you need to alter your beliefs and assumptions about networking?

THE SKILLSET for
LEVERAGING YOUR NETWORK

Building a strong and vibrant leadership network requires time and effort, but it doesn't need to overwhelm you. Once you understand how your present network is structured, who is involved, and where you can evolve your network toward being more open, diverse, and deep, you can get there quicker and easier by using these eight approaches.

LEARN FROM OTHERS

Individuals who learn by accessing others seek advice, examples, support, or instruction from people who have met a challenge similar to the one they face, or they learn how to do something by watching someone else do it. Think about who networks well in your organization or in your community. What exactly do they do, and what do they say? Try similar tactics or approaches. Ask them to talk to you about their view of networking and how they build and use relationships. Keep a networking notebook for a week. Observe people around you in meetings, working together, and in casual interactions. Who seems connected? Who seems isolated? What specifically are they doing? What clues does this activity give you about how you should act and how you should treat others?

INVITE OTHERS

Bring others into your world. Invite them to lunch. Find time for a 15- or 30-minute conversation to find out what is happening in their world and to tell them what you and your group are doing. Invite others to your meetings and ask them to contribute their expertise and their perspectives or to explore possible connections between their work and yours. Arrange one invitation each week. One week you may ask a teammate to talk for 15 minutes after a meeting and ask for an opinion on another project. The next week, you could invite a peer to lunch. Keep up the once-a-week practice and soon it will be routine.

INVITE YOURSELF

Ask to sit in on another group's meeting or planning session. Join a committee or group outside your own area. Set a goal to join a new committee or task force in the next month. If you don't know what options you have, spend a week gathering ideas. Talk to your boss, ask a peer, or check in with human resources.

ASK FOR FEEDBACK

Seek honest answers from peers, direct reports, and superiors to gain a clear picture of how you and your group function and what impact you have on others. Seeking feedback engages others in a constructive way by adding depth to existing relationships. Ask for specific comments about how others see you in regard to your relationships with others, how you share information, how you use your influence, and other networking skills.

"NETWORKING IS MARKETING. MARKETING YOURSELF, YOUR UNIQUENESS, WHAT YOU STAND FOR."
— CHRISTINE COMAFORD

WORK WITH OTHERS

Volunteer for assignments or projects that give you an opportunity to work across functions. One of the best ways to build connections with others is to work together on something. A fringe benefit is the visibility you will gain with people outside your department. Volunteer for the next assignment that involves people outside your work group. Whatever it is—a presentation to senior management, giving a plant tour, or working on a cross-functional team—raise your hand and take that step forward.

BE DIRECT

Let people know what you are doing, why it matters, and how it relates to their work or goals. By communicating clearly, you help others see how they can connect to you and your work to achieve their own goals. Talk to your direct reports about networking. Tell them you are making efforts to extend your network and that you want their input. Ask them about their projects and challenges. Make a list of people, departments, or functions that could be helpful in accomplishing their goals—seek and incorporate information from your direct reports in that list. With their help and input, make a plan that you and your direct reports can follow to create or improve your networks.

BE AN INFORMATION HUB

Develop and offer yourself as a source of information about people, processes, and facts. Increase your ability to connect with strategic information about your organization. Make a list of your information assets. What do you know? What information does your group hold? How might your information be useful to others? Make a plan to disseminate information appropriately and intentionally.

MAKE ALLIES

You may be able to develop your networking skills by working with a mentor, colleague, or coach. For a source of coaching or mentoring, look to others you see as successful leadership networkers. Interview effective networkers in your organization. Capture their specific behaviors. Ask them to observe your behaviors related to networking and to offer you feedback. You could also recruit a networking ally. The two of you could practice networking and give each other feedback, support, and encouragement.

"MY GOLDEN RULE OF NETWORKING IS SIMPLE:
DON'T KEEP SCORE."
- HARVEY MACKAY

THE TOOLSET for
LEVERAGING YOUR NETWORK:
Creating Your Network Map

Now it's time to map your own current leadership network. This diagram is a visual picture of the people you interact with to accomplish your work. Having a picture of your network in mind is the first step toward developing or improving your networking skills. In the space following.

- Draw the names of your key relationships
  (boss, direct reports, peers, customers, and so on).
- Draw double lines to those with whom you interact frequently.
- Draw single lines to people with whom you interact less frequently.
- Draw dotted lines to names of those with whom you only have rare contact.

Next, answer the following questions:

- How open, diverse, and deep is your network?
- How much do you depend upon your direct reports? People outside your scope of authority?
- What determines how much you interact with different people?

Self

KEY TAKEAWAYS in

LEVERAGING
YOUR NETWORK

BUILD A NETWORK THAT IS OPEN, DIVERSE, AND DEEP.

LEARN FROM OTHERS, INCLUDING ALLIES.

INVITE OTHERS (AND YOURSELF!).

ASK FOR FEEDBACK.

WORK WITH OTHERS.

BE DIRECT.

BE AN INFORMATION HUB.

CHAPTER NINETEEN

SEEKING EXPERIENCE

They might appear to us as strokes of genius. Testaments to courage and perseverance. Lucky accidents. Yet every discovery, innovation, and singular success we can name has a common denominator.

A person deliberately tried something new.

The spirit of exploration—an intentional willingness to immerse yourself in new and challenging situations—is what we've come to think of as seeking, which is a fundamental component of agile leadership. The pursuit of growth and expansion, the mindset, skills, and tools of the explorer, are the focus of this closing chapter.

Our premise is that effective leaders do not wait for learning opportunities to come along. They seek out and embrace them, constantly exploring new pathways for themselves and others.

Why? Because new experiences become the oxygen leaders need to be effective. Without new experiences to challenge, stretch, and inform them, leadership loses some of its essence. It's not only what they desire. It's what they need.

Another fundamental premise—that effective leaders are made and not born—suggests that seeking is not some preordained trait we possess from birth. Instead, it is a mindset that we choose, a tool we pick up, a skill we spend our life perfecting. Seekers may appear lucky, and in a profound sense, they are. But their good fortune is not by accident.

Their ability to thrive in new situations means seekers are often called upon to take on fresh challenges. The reason? They invariably say yes. More important, in the absence of new challenges being presented, they seek them out. That's no small thing. The seeking behaviors examined in this chapter require a willingness and commitment to take action—as well as considerable courage.

Before you pursue your next learning experience, consider the ten behaviors listed below that typify a leader who excels at seeking experience; identify the three that you feel you are currently strongest in and the corresponding three that you feel are most in need of development.

STRENGTH	NEED	
☐	☐	Takes advantage of opportunities to learn new things.
☐	☐	Treats all situations as an opportunity to learn something.
☐	☐	Seeks experiences that will change his or her perspective.
☐	☐	Responds well to new situations that require him/her to stretch and grow.
☐	☐	Seeks out new and diverse work experiences.
☐	☐	Takes risks in pursuit of seeking new challenges.
☐	☐	Focuses more on learning than success/failure.
☐	☐	Immerses self in new experiences.
☐	☐	Moves on when learning begins to plateau.
☐	☐	Leverages network to gain access to new learning experiences.

Take a moment to reflect on how your perceived strengths and corresponding development needs in this area have played out in the past and currently. As you progress through this chapter, keep in mind how you might augment or leverage these approaches.

> 'IF SOMEBODY OFFERS YOU AN AMAZING OPPORTUNITY
> BUT YOU ARE NOT SURE YOU CAN DO IT, SAY YES
> -THEN LEARN HOW TO DO IT LATER!'
> — RICHARD BRANSON

VOICES OF EXPERIENCE

"WHY NOT ME?"

As the Taliban's repression threatened the ability of Pakistani girls to attend school, Malala Yousafzai had been fearless in joining her classmates to speak out for their right to an education.

But the event that catapulted the issue to world attention—her diary for the BBC—might not have happened had she not sought the opportunity.

Originally, the BBC approached Malala's school seeking the insights of a teacher or an older student. All refused for fear of reprisal. It looked as if the diary, and its message to a potential audience outside Pakistan, might not happen.

That was when Malala volunteered for the project. Though she had never before written a diary, she saw the opportunity to gain broader awareness that might change the course of events.

The assassination attempt that followed only encouraged Malala to keep moving forward toward new opportunities. Following her recovery from the attempt on her life, she took her advocacy global and established the Malala Fund to provide girls educational opportunity. The money that came with a Nobel Peace Prize multiplied her experience exponentially: Malala donated the award to fund a girls' school in Pakistan.

How might you summon your courage and take risks to seek new challenges and make a difference?

THE MINDSET of
SEEKING EXPERIENCE

The fundamental mindset driving seeking behaviors is the belief that every new experience offers the potential for learning and growth. Leaders with this belief take responsibility for embracing new learning opportunities, refusing to take them for granted. Alternatively, deciding to stay in one's comfort zone and preserve the status quo of experience is seen as a lost opportunity for learning.

Beyond this core belief, some other key elements of leaders with a seeking mindset emerge.

- **THEY VENTURE OUTSIDE THEIR COMFORT ZONE—WAY OUTSIDE.** They are true believers in the aphorism that "Life begins at the edge or your comfort zone" and often find the experience of living at the edge exhilarating.

- **THEY VALUE EXPERIENCE OVER THE OUTCOMES.** The real focus is on the experience itself and what learning it might yield. This surpasses any excitement or concern with where the experience will eventually lead or its career consequences.

- **THEY TAKE OWNERSHIP.** Once committed to a new learning experience, seekers become immersed. Not content to tentatively wade in or be passive bystanders, they put themselves at the center of what's going on and take responsibility for what eventually happens.

- **THEY KNOW WHEN IT'S TIME TO MOVE ON.** Seekers are a restless lot. They want to be where the action is and sense when they are starting to become comfortable in their current situation. They would sooner run toward the next experience than run from the current one.

Exploring the anatomy of a new, challenging learning experience reveals why learning seekers are so eager to attain them. Research by CCL's Kerry Bunker and others provides a visual representation of what happens when we encounter a new learning experience.

Anatomy of a Learning Experience

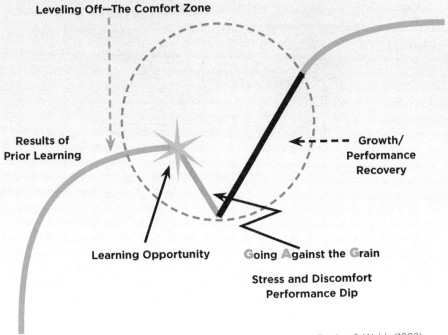

Leveling Off—The Comfort Zone

Results of
Prior Learning

Growth/
Performance
Recovery

Learning Opportunity

Going Against the Grain

Stress and Discomfort
Performance Dip

Bunker & Webb (1992)

Learning from the experiences we seek doesn't follow a continuous upward trajectory. As we assimilate learning from previous experiences, we gradually enter a leveling-off phase. New learning opportunities jolt us out of our comfort zone. Performance falters and actually decreases while we struggle to learn and apply the skills required for success in this new situation. But the decrease is only temporary. As we gain skill, pick up some wins and the confidence that comes with them, performance and growth accelerate to a higher-than-before level until, gradually, a new status quo emerges.

If we react to the new learning opportunity by choosing to stay close to our comfort zone and minimizing or avoiding exposure, we miss the discomfort of going against the grain but also the corresponding rebound in growth and performance. The end result is we are pretty much the way we were before encountering the new learning opportunity. Most striking is what doesn't happen—all of the learning that otherwise could have occurred.

Anatomy of a Lost Learning Experience

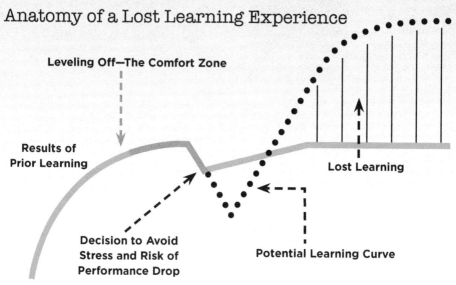

Bunker & Webb (1992)

People who are seekers recognize the value in continuously embracing learning opportunities that will propel them to ever higher levels of learning and growth. They have a knack for choosing opportunities that will yield maximum learning and further broaden their portfolio of experiences. And they do it often. This is the magic formula of high quantity, high quality, and diversity that was highlighted in Chapter 1.

Quantity speaks for itself. As for the other two variables, CCL's research has defined explicitly what seekers understand implicitly about the quality and diversity of their experiences. Let's dive a little deeper into each.

QUALITY

Quality emerges from several aspects of a learning opportunity. An exhaustive CCL study highlighted what elements of a new experience were associated with the greatest amount of learning.

- UNFAMILIAR RESPONSIBILITIES
- NEW DIRECTIONS
- INHERITED PROBLEMS
- PROBLEMS WITH EMPLOYEES
- HIGH STAKES

- SCOPE AND SCALE
- EXTERNAL PRESSURE
- INFLUENCE WITHOUT AUTHORITY
- WORK ACROSS CULTURES
- WORK-GROUP DIVERSITY

The more of these elements that are present in any one experience, the greater the potential for learning.

DIVERSITY

Beginning with the foundational Lessons of Experience study, CCL has spent decades defining the types of learning experiences we encounter. Each category (15 in all) is listed below along with a brief example.

 BOSSES AND SUPERIORS: Worked with a boss who was demanding and supportive.

 TURNAROUND: Fixed an underperforming unit or organization.

 INCREASE IN JOB SCOPE: Took on additional responsibilities without promotion.

 HORIZONTAL MOVE: Transferred/rotated to different function/job at the same level.

 NEW INITIATIVE: Created a new service/product/brand.

 PERSONAL EXPERIENCES: Played a leadership role outside the workplace.

STAKEHOLDER ENGAGEMENT: Formed a partnership or joint venture across organizations.

 ETHICAL DILEMMA: Experienced ethical violation by a superior/coworker.

 CULTURAL CROSSING: Lived and worked in another country.

 DIFFICULT PEOPLE: Handled performance problems with subordinates.

 FEEDBACK AND COACHING: Served as a mentor to someone.

 COURSEWORK AND TRAINING: Pursued advanced degree/certification.

 CRISIS: Dealt with budget or financial crisis.

 MISTAKE: Made a mistake that affected my team/unit/organization.

 CAREER SETBACK: Experienced discrimination of some sort in the workplace.

Now that you understand some fundamentals about why experience matters for learning and the quality and diversity of experiences that are out there, the rest of this chapter will introduce you to how seeking individuals make the most of new learning experiences.

THE SKILLSET of
SEEKING EXPERIENCE

Try these behavioral approaches to improve your skill at seeking. Some may require more practice than others, but all will help reframe the value of experience and orient you toward seeking quantity, quality, and diversity in new learning.

FIND THE LIMITS OF YOUR COMFORT ZONE

To get out of your comfort zone, you first have to know its boundaries. Explore both past and present circumstances to understand what experiences trigger an avoidance response in you and why. How might you reason with yourself to work past these comfort-zone traps when future situations trigger them?

TAKE RISKS

Some leaders are perfectly content to accept the status quo and remain safe. In order to become a seeker, you must be willing to accept new roles, pursue new opportunities, advocate for the unusual, and risk failing. Remember to focus more on the experience and less on the possible outcomes.

CALCULATE THE COST OF MISSED EXPERIENCES

Avoiding risk usually means that you're missing opportunity. Next time you encounter a new learning opportunity, consider what you might be missing out on if you decide not to take it. Also, what could that missed opportunity cost the organization?

LISTEN TO YOUR INTERNAL TIMER

The leveling-off phase of a learning experience is slow and gradual. Then next thing you know, you are stuck in another rut. Stay alert to when the familiarity and the safety of the status quo kick in. Ask yourself, "Am I learning anything new? Am I growing stagnant?" Know when it's time to start seeking the next new learning opportunity.

CHALLENGE YOURSELF

Identify your growth needs and then immerse yourself in situations that will push you to your limits in these areas. This may be uncomfortable and frightening at first, but it is important for you to reframe these threats as opportunities if you hope to gain the most learning from them. Seeking the first challenge is often the hardest—after seeking (and working through) repeated challenges, the confidence in knowing that you've been here before starts to grow.

SEEK OUTSIDE-OF-WORK EXPERIENCES

Learning opportunities aren't exclusive to the workplace. Sometimes new challenges outside of work are even more valuable sources of learning, filled with surprising insights. Recall the story from Chapter 1 of the individual who chose to put himself at the center of mediating a complex, emotionally charged family dispute over inherited property. The lessons he learned from this experience later proved very valuable in handling business negotiations back on the job that featured multiple parties with a lot at stake.

EXPAND YOUR NETWORK

New learning opportunities seldom just happen, and those that you seek to create for yourself can be very difficult to make a reality. Remember: It's not all up to you. Other people play a role. That's why it's important to establish a thriving network, with people who you know can make the difference in what opportunities come your way and who you can reach out to for the opportunities you are seeking. Not all networks are alike. As we discussed in the previous chapter, it is more advantageous to cultivate a network that is open, diverse, and deep.

THE TOOLSET for
SEEKING EXPERIENCE:
The Experience Audit

For seekers, success is more easily measured by the number of stamps on their passport than the plaques on their wall. They are caught up less in the constant striving for advancement and specific accomplishments and more in building an ever-expanding portfolio of experiences.

Seekers take advantage of the unique vantage point offered by their cumulative previous experience to blaze a path forward. Looking at such a leader's resume, some of their choices don't always make immediate sense and sometimes appear like zigs and zags. But beneath the surface, a story emerges. It typically involves the search for the next missing piece in their experience that will add something meaningful to everything they've already done.

The experience inventory below is a useful way to take stock of your journey to date and find that next missing piece that will provide the opportunity for challenge, learning, and growth.

Under the Quantity column, use the following scale to indicate the number of experiences you've acquired in each category.

1 = I haven't had any experiences in this category.

2 = I've had a limited number of experiences in this category.

3 = I've had a fair amount of experiences in this category.

4 = I've had too many experiences to count in this category.

Under the Quality column, use the following scale to indicate the depth of learning you've acquired in each category.

1 = I haven't had any meaningful learning in this category.

2 = I've learned a limited number of things from my experiences in this category.

3 = I've learned a fair amount from my experiences in this category.

4 = I could write a book based on what I've learned from my experiences in this category.

	QUANTITY	QUALITY
Bosses and superiors		
Turnaround		
Increase in job scope		
Horizontal move		
New initiative		
Personal experiences		
Stakeholder engagement		
Ethical dilemma		
Cultural crossing		
Difficult people		
Feedback and coaching		
Coursework and training		

Take a moment to reflect on the significant learning experiences that you've had and look for patterns and themes. For example, are there any areas where you see large discrepancies between the ratings for quantity and quality of experience?

Next, consider what types of experiences are missing and what you might gain from seeking them out. What is the next missing piece that will enrich your existing portfolio of experiences?

"I DON'T KNOW WHERE I'M GOING FROM HERE,
BUT I PROMISE IT WON'T BE BORING."
- DAVID BOWIE

KEY TAKEAWAYS in

SEEKING EXPERIENCE

VENTURE OUTSIDE YOUR COMFORT ZONE.

VALUE EXPERIENCE
OVER POTENTIAL OUTCOMES.

TAKE OWNERSHIP AND
IMMERSE YOURSELF.

KNOW WHEN IT'S TIME TO MOVE ON.

WEIGH OPPORTUNITY COSTS.

SEEK LEARNING EXPERIENCES
OUTSIDE OF WORK.

SEEK QUANTITY, QUALITY, AND DIVERSITY
IN YOUR EXPERIENCES.

THE JOURNEY CONTINUES:
YOUR PATH TO BECOMING AN EXPERIENCE-DRIVEN LEADER

Reprising a theme from the beginning of this book, experience is an opportunity but only when we capitalize on it. With the knowledge, insight, and skill you've acquired, you now have everything you need to make the opportunity of experience your own and leverage it to the fullest.

It's not enough to have a great opportunity before you. As you've no doubt realized, making the most of your experience involves hard work and, at times, some pain and sacrifice. You need to have a strong motivation to invest the time and effort necessary to become an experience-driven leader. It needs to mean something to you personally.

So take a moment to ask yourself what you will gain as a result of applying, practicing, and refining the mindsets, skillsets, and toolsets featured in this book? How will they change you as a leader? As a person? What will they enable you to do that you haven't done before? How will they lead to different results for your career, team, and organization?

Identify those things you might gain that resonate with you most strongly and make sure your efforts at developing and growing your experience-driven leadership skills bring you closer to achieving them.

When you're ready to set some goals, keep these time-tested, research-based fundamentals in mind.

FOCUS!

When you're motivated and excited to develop and change, the temptation is to take on a bunch of things at once. Well-intentioned? Yes. Ambitious? Yes. A recipe for success? Hardly. Focus your efforts on a select few areas (maybe even one) that will really yield an impact and tap into your underlying energy and passion. Now you're heading in the right direction. But not so fast. Consider what you're getting into. How hard will it be to change? How long will it take? A quick reality check might lead to identifying an area of focus that, while still challenging, has a better chance of success associated with it.

CHOOSE THE RIGHT KIND OF GOAL

Different goals fit different purposes. Three in particular are relevant to developing what you've learned about experience-driven leadership.

- BEHAVIORAL GOALS CHANGE HOW YOU ACT.

- COMPETENCY GOALS IMPROVE A SKILL.

- OUTCOME GOALS MEET A TARGET.

One type of goal is not better than another. Just consider which goal is the most appropriate for the area of focus you've chosen.

HAVE A PLAN

It seems obvious, but a lot of people just go straight to doing. Yes, that's consistent with sensemaking and some of the other skills we've highlighted, but it doesn't apply as well to intentional, goal-focused behavior change. No need to get too fancy. A solid plan should include the following four elements:

- TACTICS: THE SPECIFIC STEPS YOU WILL TAKE.

- RESOURCES: WHAT YOU NEED TO MAKE THE CHANGE.

- TRACKING: MEASURING IS KEY TO MAKING PROGRESS AND RECALIBRATING WHEN NECESSARY.

- CELEBRATING: THAT'S RIGHT. YOU'VE EARNED IT!

DEAL WITH OBSTACLES

Things will go wrong. Let's repeat. Things will go wrong. Anticipate it. Have a plan. Learn from what happened. And most importantly, don't get discouraged. Pick yourself up, get your bearings and keep moving ahead.

TAKE ACTION!
MORE ON THAT NEXT.

CONNECTING GOALS TO YOUR LEADERSHIP JOURNEY

To tie this together, here are three more tools that will help you with the critical task of putting your goals into action. An element common to each is staying focused on building your development as an experience-driven leader into your day-to-day activities. That way, your development isn't separate from your work. It is your work.

TOOL #1
LINKING to Your
KEY LEADERSHIP CHALLENGE

Applying your development efforts in the context of a key leadership challenge is an excellent way to galvanize your efforts. To identify the right leadership challenge, consider the following criteria. Your key challenge:

- SHOULD BE OF PRIMARY IMPORTANCE TO YOU.
- SHOULD INVOLVE OTHERS WHO ARE INVESTED IN THE OUTCOME.
- SHOULD BE ONE THAT HAS PERSISTED FOR SOME TIME.
- MIGHT REQUIRE SIGNIFICANT CHANGE IN VALUES, ASSUMPTIONS, OR BEHAVIORS OF THOSE INVOLVED.

Examples of a key leadership challenge may include

- GAINING BUY-IN FOR A CHALLENGING REVENUE GOAL FOR THE SALES TEAM.
- SECURING BUDGET AND BOARD APPROVAL FOR A NEW INITIATIVE.
- LEADING A CHANGE INITIATIVE.
- MERGING DEPARTMENTS WITH A NEW GROUP.
- BEING SHORT-STAFFED AND NEEDING TO COMPLETE A HEAVY WORKLOAD.

Take a moment to identify a leadership situation or challenge where you are being called upon to use your best leadership skills.

DESCRIBE THE SITUATION BRIEFLY BELOW.

....

....

....

....

IDENTIFY THE SPECIFIC CHALLENGE.
("HOW DO I . . ." OR "HOW AM I GOING TO . . .")

....

....

....

....

HOW WILL THIS CHALLENGE PROVIDE OPPORTUNITIES TO ENGAGE IN BEHAVIORS THAT WILL HELP YOU ACHIEVE YOUR DEVELOPMENTAL GOALS?

....

....

....

....

TOOL #2
LEVERAGING Your
ACCOUNTABILITY PARTNER

At this point, you should have a clearer sense of where you need to focus your energies to become an experience-driven leader. It's important that you take ownership of this, but of course it's a much easier and more productive task when you've got someone in your corner. We recommend partnering with a manager or peer to hold you accountable, using this commitment as a motivational tool. Your accountability partner should:

- HAVE INSIGHT INTO YOUR GOALS.

- BE ABLE TO PROVIDE CRITICAL FEEDBACK IN ADDITION TO SUPPORT.

- HAVE AN OPPORTUNITY TO CHECK IN WITH YOU ON A TIMELY BASIS.

Consider now some of the key things you would like to address in your development and specifically how your accountability partner might best support you.

DEVELOPMENT OBJECTIVE/GOAL ....

....

....

HOW MY ACCOUNTABILITY PARTNER CAN SUPPORT ME

....

....

....

TOOL #3
DEVELOPING
ON THE JOB

We define development in place as adding challenges (at work and outside work) that broaden your portfolio of leadership experiences. These opportunities don't only come in terms of major promotions or job changes. You can also seek out significant learning opportunities as part of your current role, laying the groundwork of experience. For example, when you take on high-stakes assignments, tight deadlines, or unfamiliar tasks that a boss delegates to you, these experiences prepare you for new roles in the future.

Consider these questions when evaluating development-in-place opportunities:

- HOW CAN THIS CHALLENGE HELP ME ACHIEVE MY DEVELOPMENTAL GOAL?

- WHAT ARE THE MINDSET, SKILLS, AND TOOLS I NEED TO PRACTICE?

- WHAT ARE THE SUPPORT MECHANISMS I NEED, AND WHO CAN PROVIDE THEM?

The road ahead of you is long and will have twists and turns. All the better. That's the nature of learning from experience. It's more about the journey itself than the destination. And the missteps and misadventures along the way offer some of the greatest opportunities for learning and growth.

So keep moving on your journey. Drawing from the past. Fully realizing the present. Looking ahead. Stay on the journey long enough that your ability to capitalize on experience becomes more than just a set of skills. It becomes a way of life.

ABOUT THE CENTER FOR CREATIVE LEADERSHIP

The Center for Creative Leadership (CCL) is a top-ranked global provider of leadership development. By leveraging the power of leadership to drive results that matter most to clients, CCL transforms individual leaders, teams, organizations, and society. Our array of cutting-edge solutions is steeped in extensive research and experience gained from working with hundreds of thousands of leaders at all levels. Ranked among the world's Top 5 providers of executive education by *Financial Times* and in the Top 10 by *Bloomberg BusinessWeek*, CCL has offices in Greensboro, North Carolina; Colorado Springs, Colorado; San Diego, California; Brussels, Belgium; Moscow, Russia; Addis Ababa, Ethiopia; Johannesburg, South Africa; Singapore; Gurgaon, India; and Shanghai, China.

Center for
Creative
Leadership·

READY TO TAKE THE NEXT STEP
WITH *LEAD 4 SUCCESS*?

Visit ccl.org to learn about additional ways you can learn more and apply the Fundamental Four. Plus, if you think your organization might benefit from a more hands on approach to the concepts covered in the *Lead 4 Success* book, visit ccl.org/l4s to learn more about program availability or licensing. CCL's *Lead 4 Success* program is a two-day experience aimed at helping you understand, practice, and apply the Fundamental Four to your specific challenges. The *Lead 4 Success* book and two-day program have both been developed by the Center for Creative Leadership, a top-ranked, global provider of leadership development and research that delivers results that matter for individuals, teams, organizations, and society as a whole. A portion of the cost of this book and the program funds the ongoing research and development of underserved populations around the world.

GRATITUDE

With appreciation, the author acknowledges the contributors to the following CCL Press publications used as primary sources for *Lead 4 Success*:

Been, R. (2016). Personal correspondence.

Bunker, K. A., & Wakefield, M. (2005). *Leading with authenticity in times of transition.* Greensboro, NC: Center for Creative Leadership.

Bunker, K. A., & Webb, A. D. (1992). *Learning how to learn from experience: Impact of stress and coping.* Greensboro, NC: Center for Creative Leadership.

Cartwright, T., & Baldwin, D. (2006). *Communicating your vision.* Greensboro, NC: Center for Creative Leadership.

Center for Creative Leadership. *Benchmarks by Design.* (2015). [Assessment]. Greensboro, NC: Center for Creative Leadership.

Center for Creative Leadership. *Benchmarks for Learning Agility.* (2015). [Assessment]. Greensboro, NC: Center for Creative Leadership.

Center for Creative Leadership. *Creating a vision: Lead 2.0 package.* (2014). [E-learning tool]. Greensboro, NC: Center for Creative Leadership.

Center for Creative Leadership. *Selling yourself without selling out: Lead 2.0 package.* (2014). [E-learning tool] Greensboro, NC: Center for Creative Leadership.

Center for Creative Leadership (2013). *Creating your leadership brand: Intention + impact.* [Slide Presentation]. Greensboro, NC: Center for Creative Leadership.

Criswell, C., & Campbell, D. (2008). *Building an authentic leadership image.* Greensboro, NC: Center for Creative Leadership.

Gentry, W. A., & Leslie, J. B. (2012). *Developing political savvy.* Greensboro, NC: Center for Creative Leadership.

Grayson, C., & Baldwin, D. (2007). *Leadership networking: Connect, collaborate, create.* Greensboro, NC: Center for Creative Leadership.

Hallenbeck, G. (2014, April 8). Hardship: A different kind of challenge. [Web log post]. Retrieved from https://www.ccl.org/blog/hardship-a-different-kind-of-challenge/.

Hallenbeck, G. (2016). *Learning agility: Unlock the lessons of experience.* Greensboro, NC: Center for Creative Leadership.

Hannum, K. M. (2007). *Social identity: Knowing yourself, leading others.* Greensboro, NC: Center for Creative Leadership.

Hernez-Broome, G., McLaughlin, C., & Trovas, S. (2006). *Selling yourself without selling out: A leader's guide to ethical self-promotion.* Greensboro, NC: Center for Creative Leadership.

Hoppe, M. H. (2014). *Active listening: Improve your ability to listen and lead.* Greensboro, NC: Center for Creative Leadership.

Horth, D. M., Miller, L. B., & Mount, P. R. (2016). *Leadership brand: Deliver on your promise.* Greensboro, NC: Center for Creative Leadership.

Kirkland, K., & Manoogian, S. (1998). *Ongoing feedback: How to get it, how to use it.* Greensboro, NC: Center for Creative Leadership.

Reinhold, D., Patterson, T. & Hegel, P. (2015). *Make learning stick: Best practices to get the most out of leadership development.* [White Paper]. Greensboro, NC: Center for Creative Leadership.

Scisco, P., McCauley, C. D., Leslie, J. B., & Elsey, R. (2014). *Change now! Five steps to better leadership.* Greensboro, NC: Center for Creative Leadership.

Wei, R. R., & Yip, J. (2008). *Leadership wisdom: Discovering the lessons of experience.* Greensboro, NC: Center for Creative Leadership.

Weitzel, S. R. (2000). *Feedback that works: How to build and deliver your message.* Greensboro, NC: Center for Creative Leadership.

Wilburn, P., & Cullen, K. (2014). *A leader's network: How to help your talent invest in the right relationships at the right time.* [White Paper]. Greensboro, NC: Center for Creative Leadership.

Yip, J., Ernst, C., & Campbell, M. (2009). *Boundary spanning leadership: Mission critical perspectives from the executive suite.* [White Paper]. Greensboro, NC: Center for Creative Leadership.

The author acknowledges the authors of the following works, which informed its insights regarding identity and networking:

Burt, R. S. (1992). *Structural holes. The social structure of competition.* Cambridge, MA: Harvard University Press.

Cross, R., Ernst, C., & Pasmore, W. (2013). A bridge too far? How boundary spanning net-works drive organizational change and effectiveness. *Organizational Dynamics, 42*(2), 81–91.

Cross, R. L., & Parker, A. (2004). *The hidden power of social networks: Understanding how work really gets done in organizations.* Watertown, MA: Harvard Business Press.

Cross, R., Thomas, R. J., & Light, D. A. (2008). How top talent uses networks and where rising stars get trapped. *Organizational Dynamics, 37*(2), 165–180.

Ernst, C., & Chrobot-Mason, D. (2010). *Boundary spanning leadership: Six practices for solving problems, driving innovation, and transforming organizations.* New York, NY: McGraw-Hill Professional.

Tajfel, H., & Turner, J. (1979). An integrative theory of intergroup conflict. In W. G. Austin & S. Worchel (Eds.), *The social psychology of intergroup relations,* (pp. 33–47). Belmont, CA: Wadsworth.

CPSIA information can be obtained
at www.ICGtesting.com
Printed in the USA
BVOW05s2139250717

489653BV00024B/46/P

9 781604 916447